READING
the
WATER

MARK HUME

READING
the
WATER

FLY FISHING,
FATHERHOOD, AND
FINDING STRENGTH
IN NATURE

GREYSTONE BOOKS
Vancouver/Berkeley/London

Greystone Books Ltd.
greystonebooks.com

Cataloguing data available from Library and Archives Canada
ISBN 978-1-77164-569-0 (cloth)
ISBN 978-1-77164-570-6 (epub)

Editing by Paula Ayer
Proofreading by Alison Strobel
Jacket and text design by Belle Wuthrich
Jacket images by A-Digit / iStock;
    tanya_morozz and Sutthithep Kaensuwan / Shutterstock
Interior images by Evgeniy Zotov and A-Digit / iStock;
    PavloArt Studio / Shutterstock

Printed in Canada on FSC® certified paper at Friesens. The FSC® label means that materials used for the product have been responsibly sourced.

Greystone Books gratefully acknowledges the Musqueam, Squamish, and Tsleil-Waututh peoples on whose land our Vancouver head office is located.

Greystone Books thanks the Canada Council for the Arts, the British Columbia Arts Council, the Province of British Columbia through the Book Publishing Tax Credit, and the Government of Canada for supporting our publishing activities.

Canada

*This book is dedicated to
Maggie, Emma, and Claire, who traveled with me,
and it is offered in memory of Father Charles Brandt
and Van Egan, friends who once walked the streams
I walked, searching for the fish I sought.*

*With special thanks to editor Paula Ayer and
publisher Rob Sanders, both at Greystone Books,
whose faith in me made this possible.*

CONTENTS

INTRODUCTION

TROUT AND SALMON USE a calibration of light, magnetism, and the scent of water to find their way home. People use memories and dreams. Both get lost sometimes.

Looking back on the map of my life I see the waypoints clearly enough, none more vivid or transformational than the experience of becoming a father. When I first gazed into the faces of my daughters, moments after each was born, I saw pale, liquid blue eyes struggling to focus and find their place in the world. I knew that helping them find their footing, their path through the forest, would be my struggle too. I wasn't sure how to guide them but felt somehow the knowledge would come naturally, and that it would involve bestowing on them the blessing of water and of fish.

My bond with fishing began when, at seven years old, I went seeking the source of a small mountain stream, where I found a trout that seemed to have always been waiting for me. From that point I never stopped searching in water, not just for hidden fish but for answers, for emotional renewal and strength.

Over the years I evolved from catching trout with my hands to using a bobber and worm, and from there went on to the slightly more involved method of casting flashing, bright lures on a spinning rod. Then inextricably, I was drawn to the complexity of fly fishing, to its intricacies, rituals, and poetry. As a boy I did not have anyone to show me how it was done. So I read books, and when I encountered fly fishers on the water I would stand back, watching from a distance as they threw long, sinuous lines arcing through the air. Once I saw that graceful form of casting, I knew I had to do it too. I felt compelled to understand the mystery.

I soon learned that fly fishing is more than just a pastime; it is a place of solace, a way of learning and of teaching. Done right, fly fishing is a meditation; a way of questing after truths in nature—and in yourself.

When I became a father I knew I would guide Emma and Claire along riverbanks, show them how to wade on rocks worn smooth by fluvial erosion, teach them how to read the water and how to cast with elegance. Those lessons on technique would be relatively easy to give, but I didn't know if a love of fishing, which had fallen to me as a kind of natural inheritance, could be taught. I thought it important to try, however, because fly fishing for me had become a way of navigating life, and I wanted that for them too. Through an absorbing involvement in nature, fly fishing fosters resilience and inner strength. It can help make a person whole. I felt my daughters should know that, though I wasn't aware at the beginning of our journey together how much teaching them to fish would help me; how I would draw strength from them too.

———

FLY FISHING IS AN INTENSELY observational way of experiencing the world, and in that sense it is a spiritual experience. Its adherents often describe it as being more of a religion than a sport, and perhaps it is, for there is a profound, ancient human connection between water, fish, and faith. The ichthus—two intersecting arcs that form a depiction of a fish—is one of the earliest symbols of Christianity. And baptism, the sacrament of admission to the Christian church, the path to salvation, is achieved through immersion in water. In Shintoism the purification ritual before entering a shrine includes bathing your hands and cleansing your mouth with water, and similar practices are followed in Islam, Judaism, and Sikhism. Many Indigenous cultures in North America recognize the mystical power of water by using it in ceremonies related to puberty, marriage, birth, and death. And in Taoism water is a metaphor for life, in which we are seen as being like rivers flowing irresistibly to something larger. So in almost all major religions there is a powerful connection to water, a liquid that erodes and is absorbed, that penetrates rock and forms human bones, that falls from the heavens, rises from the earth—and is the domain of fish, creatures which to me hold infinite fascination. To know the fish, you must catch the fish, and to catch the fish, you must know the water. Those who fish wade in rivers, ponder the depths of lakes, and drift with ocean tides. In the process of searching, they develop a reverence for the virtues of nature; they reawaken in themselves an awareness of what it means to fit in to the universe.

Fly fishing taught me how to move purposefully on trout streams and steelhead rivers, on creeks and ponds where bass and pike lay hidden in the shadows. I slipped into a state of grace carrying a fly rod, and I came to appreciate that there is something wonderful, magical, revelatory, about drawing fish into the light. I wanted my daughters to see that with the wave of a fly rod they could make the invisible visible, divining creatures of astonishing beauty into existence.

A wild trout is as bright as a wildflower, and holding one is a remarkable experience. At that moment nothing else exists, and I felt Emma and Claire needed to encounter that, to understand that enduring beauty could be found in nature, even as the world they were inheriting, and I was leaving, seemed to be unraveling around them.

In my short lifetime I have seen great rivers dammed, entire forests clearcut, species pushed to the verge of extinction, and the planet's climate compromised to the point it has become threatening. And yet, there on the water, reaching down to touch a cold-blooded fish, I have always found hope. As my daughters awakened and began to see the Earth changing, I knew they would need that kind of connection to nature if they were going to have faith that the planet could be saved—and restored.

When I began fishing I was often alone on the water. But as soon as my daughters were old enough to learn they began going with me. At first they just took turns holding my rod as I rowed slowly around a lake. Emma, serious and determined, always wanted a turn at the oars so she could control the boat, while Claire, joyful and contemplative, was content hanging over the side to gently crease the water with her fingertips. Sometimes they would perch together at the bow, looking down at the reflection of the sky, their arms outstretched as if they were flying, and urging me to row faster. As they grew older I taught them casting techniques, how to tie blood knots, and which flies to select. I taught them how to study currents to understand where a trout might lie in a stream.

But I knew for them to reach enlightenment as fly fishers, to learn how to honor life by being bound to nature, ultimately the fish would have to teach them—just as the fish had taught me.

———

A HUMAN LIFE GOES THROUGH changes, like a river. It springs to existence in the headwaters, gathers strength from its tributaries, floods its banks, cuts new pathways through the erodible earth, and then subsides into a greater presence, a sea in which its turbidity settles and the water seeks to regain the clarity it had in the beginning.

This memoir deals with the transformative importance of fly fishing in my life. It is about discovering the secrets of water as a boy, and as a father passing on that legacy to my young daughters. Going deep into nature with me in pursuit of trout and salmon helped shape them, as I hoped it would. What I didn't expect was how much the experience would shape me too, developing a bond that allowed me to draw strength from them, to see that in times of darkness, there is always a path to light.

I cannot say that this is all that happened, or that it all happened exactly this way, but this is how I remember a part of my life, connected by a thread of fishing line and shaped by water.

I

HEADWATERS

"We have to fall in love with the natural world.
We only save something if we love it, and
we only love it if we think it is sacred."

FATHER CHARLES BRANDT,
hermit priest of the Oyster River

THE
WATERSHED

I WAS NOT TAUGHT to read the waters. It came to me naturally, the way poetry or dance or dreams come to others, and it came to me early.

When I was seven, before I learned anything about fishing, and before I knew a nearby creek contained trout, I was intrigued by the mountain that rose above the pastoral landscape where we lived in the Okanagan Valley. Our stately farmhouse, which stood at the end of a long dirt driveway with an ancient apricot tree shading the back door, rested in a vast orchard of apple, peach, and cherry trees that bloomed pink and white in spring and glistened with red and yellow fruit in late summer. Beyond the orchards, Campbell Mountain, stratified with green forest and dry, brown bunchgrass, stood at the edge of our world. It leaned back from the valley, forming a wild, scarred backdrop to the linear, fertile agricultural land below.

I had four brothers, two older, two younger. Timothy, who was just two years older, would sometimes tolerate my presence, and we shared an interest in wild things. We both looked up at the mountain with wonder. Our eldest brother, Stephen, had hiked there with friends, and we wanted to go too. We told our mother we were off exploring, and ran into the carefully manicured orchards. She was distracted with a new baby, children running everywhere, a garden to tend, chickens to feed, and a goat to milk, so she didn't know we were going well beyond our yard to see what we could find.

To get to the mountain we hiked through the orderly ranks of fruit trees until we reached what seemed to be the borderline of civilization—a narrow flume, snaking along the slope as far as we could see in either direction. It divided the hard pine forest, crackling with summer heat on the mountainside above, from the soft, verdant orchards, growing heavy with fruit on the flat benchland below.

Above was the wild, home to rattlesnakes and burrowing owls. Below lay the quilted garden where high-stepping quail ran and the most dangerous animal was a farmer's dog, or sometimes the farmer. We knew of one old man who protected his cherry trees from raiding kids by firing shotgun shells loaded with coarse salt instead of buckshot.

I had wanted to go high up the mysterious, slumbering mountain I could see from my bedroom window. But now that we were up there in the dry heat, with the luxuriant orchards laid out below, I had a new perspective of my small world, and realized what I really wanted was to go back down into the valley. To go down to where the water ran.

Penticton Creek, which I had seen before only from a bridge as the family drove to town, lay like a shining ribbon across the landscape. It came out of a small valley behind Campbell Mountain, cut through the terraces, and flowed into Okanagan Lake, a shining, azure body of water eighty miles long, where Ogopogo, a fish-eating creature with a horselike head and a snake's body, is said to live in the depths, occasionally rising up to ripple the surface and stir imaginations.

The creek's course was marked by a dark-green, tangled layer of vegetation; wherever the stream went, unruly life flourished. There was something magnetic and compelling that drew me to it. I wanted to see where it began.

"Let's follow the flume," I said to Tim, figuring the water in the metal trough and the stream in the valley must flow from the same source. "We have to find out where it comes from."

So a quest began. Without knowing it I gave in to the first of many spells cast by moving water: the need to find the headwaters, the source.

We clambered up, walking on the wooden crossbeams over the flume as if they were railway ties. Below our feet the irrigation water sparkled and raced toward the patient, thirsty orchards.

On the mountain slope, cracked open by old outwash ravines and gnarled by exposed bedrock, we saw tawny mule deer vaulting through the forest, the does delicate beside the thick-necked bucks, which stopped to look back and display their antlers. A badger, shaggy, languid, and dangerous as a loaded gun, basked in the sun outside the dark entrance to its den. Not knowing if it would flee or attack us, we crouched and whispered past it without being seen.

The air on the mountainside was different, not soft and sweet like in the orchards but fragrant with the sharp smell of ponderosa pines and thatches of brittle bunchgrass where cactus nested. We heard the soft buzz of Northern Pacific rattlers and saw them lounging on rocky ledges in the sun. When poked with a stick, they curled their muscular, tan-colored bodies, and their rattles emitted an angry hiss. Red-tailed hawks spiraled above, wings draped, piercing the sky with harsh, keening calls that over a lifetime I would learn to hear as a lament for all the wild things threatened or lost. At that moment the cry of the hawk was the soundtrack of wild mystery.

The flume, built by the Southern Okanagan Land Company to promote land sales in 1906, was on a trestle set at a slight, steady pitch, allowing the same force that keeps the moon in orbit around Earth to propel the water down to the terraces. Ahead we could see the flume slowly converging with the valley bottom and Penticton Creek. A meeting of the waters lay ahead, a confluence. We hurried along the ragged mountainside until we found where the flume came from. It was a startling sight: there was a dam across the stream. The creek ended at a massive concrete wall, a seamless barricade. Behind the dam, guarded by a chain-link fence and "No Trespassing" signs, lay the city's drinking water reservoir. At the base of the dam, its blunt face stained wet with spillover, was a black plunge pool, its surface painted with an unfolding filigree of white foam.

It was cold in the shadow of the dam, which blotted out not just the movement of the wild stream but the sunlight itself. The dark water that lay at its base seemed lifeless. Ahead of us the flume emerged from under a fence. But peering through the mesh, we could see the water came from inside the dam, a single, glinting, black filament flowing toward us and daylight.

So we went into the darkness.

Clambering down into the flume between the wooden ties, stepping into fast, ankle-deep water, we ducked under

the barrier, ignoring the "No Trespassing" sign. Mist saturated the air and the tunnel echoed with the crashing sounds
of lake monsters. I thought, this must be what it's like to live
submerged, breathing underwater like a fish.

When our eyes adjusted, we saw a small pool in the dim
light. And that's where we found the trout, entrained in a
settling pond at the head of the flume. The fish couldn't swim
upstream because the water pouring down the tunnel from
the dam was too fast, and downstream they sensed danger
in the flume, where the water was so shallow it would barely
cover them. So they stayed in the pool, moving in a tight,
interlaced school, collecting like gold in a seam, waiting to
be discovered. When we stepped into the pool the trout separated, dashing around us, bumping against our legs. I tried
to grab the darting fish, but they shot from my hands, slick as
polished stones. Tim scooped some up, trapping them against
a shelf, so I herded more fish toward him, whooping and slapping the water in little-boy bedlam. After a few minutes the
last of the excited school of trout had vanished, foot-long fish
somehow compressing into nothingness in the shadows.

But by then Tim had caught four silver, speckled brook
trout, tossing them out of the water, where they flapped
before gasping and lying still. He brought them home dangling from their gills on a forked willow stick, as a present
for our mother, who loved harvesting wild things, making
tea out of rose hips and collecting watercress along streams.

They were the first trout I had seen and I was captivated
by their beauty. They seemed hand-painted, daubed with
surprising colors. They had olivaceous backs of dusky yel-
lowish green, olive vermiculations, bloodred spots circled
with blue, and winter-white bellies. Our journey had led to

a treasure and it was astonishing to see such perfect form, such vividness, emerging so unexpectedly from the water.

It was magic, cast by the water, spun by the mist.

———

FROM THEN ON I BEGAN to dream about Penticton Creek and catching its hidden, bejeweled trout. I felt drawn to the water, drawn to the fish.

All that summer my older brothers and their friends went to the stream to fish and to swim. While they lay sunning on warm rocks, I crept through thickets of willows along the banks, peering into the water, studying the movement of trout within the movement of the stream.

The fish lay in deep pools where I couldn't reach them, but the older boys taught me to throw rocks, scattering the trout in a spray of panic. The fish fled the safety of deep water, darting upstream, doubling back, changing direction again, their tails propelling them with astonishing speed—until the pool stood empty. Somehow the brook trout had disappeared.

I tried again, throwing rocks into another pool, and the same thing happened. The trout darted about for a moment—then they were just gone.

But where were they hiding? I couldn't see them in the shallow water at the head of the pool, where water spilled down an impassable slope. During the 1940s a flood-control program had turned sections of the free-flowing creek into a series of terraced pools linked by concrete spillways. The natural rapids had been paved out of existence. In high spring water, trout could slide down the spillways, going from pool to pool, but they could not move back upstream because the water was too shallow, the inclines too steep.

So where did the fish in the pools go when they fled the rocks we threw?

The older boys told me the trout darted into crevices and I might catch them there, with my hands. Wading in search of the vanished trout I saw the current had scoured holes at the base of the concrete cap, where the structure lay heavy against the native streambed. And that's where the frightened trout went. They raced across the shallows and darted into holes bored by water and by swirling bits of sand.

Knee-deep in the stream I moved along the base of the spillway, groping inside, sometimes catching trout as they tried to dash out, but often just feeling them flash past: cold, bright surges of electricity in the water. With my fingers spread like a net I searched the crevices, blindly feeling for fish, trying to read with my fingertips the braille of the streambed, hoping for a smooth, icy trout in the small caves cut into the concrete.

My skill increased with each trip to the stream. Every time I caught a fish I wanted to catch another. And soon I was coming home from the creek with strings of four or five trout, all caught by hand. My mom was pleased to have fresh trout for dinner, and I, proud provider, just wanted to catch more fish and bigger fish. I ran to Penticton Creek whenever I could during the summer.

Fishing alone one afternoon in bright sunlight I began to explore a stretch of water that was new to me. I found where the current had whirled stones on the bottom, creating dark pockets. I probed the first carefully and a foot-long trout bolted out, darted between my legs, and disappeared downstream. I worked my way to the next hole, spread my fingers to form a net, and reached into the darkness. I felt an effortless slice of flesh, followed instantly by the sensation of a sharp edge cutting through to gristle and to bone. A shard of glass that was hiding where a glinting trout should have been. When I drew out my hand, dark blood streamed down my left arm and fell in globs that spun in the current around my legs.

Some people like to say that fishing is in their veins. For me this is a recurring image: my blood mixed with the water of a trout stream, drifting away as red as the backs of spawning kokanee.

I walked home with my hand held tight against my chest, wrapped in my T-shirt sopping with dark water and blood.

"Oh, goodness, what have you done?" asked my mother when I stood at the door, reluctant to come in and drip on her clean kitchen floor.

When a doctor stitched the wound, he remarked that it was unusual I didn't cry, but I felt only a dull throb. The pain seemed internal, wandering somewhere in my body. What hurt wasn't so much the cut, but the realization my relationship with the creek, and the magical brook trout it held, had changed.

I knew the current must have dropped more broken glass among the river stones, jagged pieces that lay razor-edge up. I imagined the fragments, as transparent as water, lying hidden and waiting. And I knew that I couldn't plunge my hand blindly into dark holes anymore. As I looked at the purple wound bristling with black stitches, I knew I would have to learn how to catch trout with a fishing rod.

I didn't have a rod. But somehow I had to get one, because turning away from the creek was unthinkable. I was hooked when I saw that first trout pulled from the flume, and bleeding into the creek water had been an even more binding experience. Friends had taught me that. In a boyhood ritual we cut our fingers, pressed them together, and then we were blood brothers.

So I knew a bond was formed the day I reached into the lightless chamber at the bottom of the stream. When I felt glass slicing me, and saw my blood streaming away with the current, like yarn pulled by a threading hook, I was woven into the water and it into me.

Sixty years later I still have the scar curling over a knuckle on the middle finger of my left hand. It is faded now, but I can make out the smooth white line with stitch marks.

It looks like the skeleton of a small fish.

And it records the beginning of my journey.

READING
THE WATER

A FEW WEEKS AFTER I cut myself fishing with my hands I got a small fiberglass rod with a level wind reel for my birthday. To cast, I held loops of loose line in one hand, and with a swing, I could throw a weighted hook several feet. I practiced on the lawn, casting for hours into my upturned baseball cap while the trees swayed in the wind and clouds streamed overhead. My brothers had little patience for this and called on me to play catch by kicking a football, to play tag, to play guns. But all I really cared about was getting the weight on the end of my line to drop into the frayed red hat.

Our rambling old house, built in the early 1900s, sat on benchlands above the small town of Penticton, which celebrated the twin foundations of its economy—tourism and farming—with an annual peach festival. My parents were recent immigrants from England who had met during the Second World War and married shortly after—she a member of the Women's Land Army, stationed at a farm in Southport, on the Irish Sea, and he a conscientious objector interned there after refusing to fight. They were both Christadelphians, a strictly pacifist group outside the mainstream Christian doctrine, and after the war they came to Canada—a young country that offered fresh beginnings. In 1956, after short stays in several communities on Vancouver Island, my family had moved to the fruit basket of the Okanagan Valley, where my father worked as editor of the *Penticton Herald*, a small daily where reporters clattered out their urgent stories on heavy, old Remington typewriters. Newspapering was his life, and around the dinner table he would tell us of the stories he thought would interest us: of the boy who'd lost his fingers in a lawn mower accident, or the farmer who had been fined for dragging a dead horse through city streets on his way to the dump. One night he told us of a great forest fire burning in the valley and of how government agents had swept through local beer parlors, telling all able-bodied young men that they were now firefighters. He seemed to work in a dangerous and exciting world; one I could hardly imagine and which consumed most of his time. We didn't fish together then, didn't hike together, didn't play catch or go camping, and my life was as much a mystery to him as his was to me.

Our family had grown to include five boys: Stephen, the oldest, followed by Timothy, me in the middle, Andrew, and Jonathan. My mother let all but the youngest run free in the orchards that surrounded our home, and we developed a love of nature through the walks she took us on, collecting bird nests, seedpods, and wild plants. At night she read us Beatrix Potter books, telling us the British author shared her maiden name. "She might be a distant auntie," she said, obviously delighted by the possibility. To me that meant Peter Rabbit, Jemima Puddle-Duck, and Mr. Jeremy Fisher, who went fishing on a lily pad until he was almost swallowed by a giant trout, were somehow related to us. It was easy for me to imagine my mother, a gentle woman who talked to her chickens, praising them for their eggs, and who brought her goat into the kitchen to milk it, as coming from a place where the animals spoke and had wonderful adventures.

While the other boys developed passions for sports and art, kite flying and climbing to the highest branches of swaying trees, my interests lay elsewhere. I heard the song of the water and each summer dreamed only of slipping away through the orchard to Penticton Creek.

———

THE FRUIT TREES—MCINTOSH, RED DELICIOUS, and Transparents, flanked by groves of Bing cherries and Redhaven peaches—stood in long, sedate rows around our home. The trees were so neatly laid out the seedlings seemed to have been planted with a mason's string line. In spring they burst into bloom, petals glowing like the embers of a fireworks display, pollen drifting like ash, saturating the air with fragrance.

Between the orchards were stone fences, built in the late 1800s and early 1900s as farmers cleared the land, marking boundaries with rocks dropped by retreating glaciers. Wildflowers and bunches of asparagus sprouted amid the hand-piled stones.

Prior to World War I irrigation systems were built in the valley, using gravity to bring water down from the hills. That allowed the parched terraces that had grown mostly tumbleweed, black sage, and cactus to be turned into lush orchards. The gravity-fed flume on Campbell Mountain was the central part of that irrigation system for several decades, through the 1950s, but it gradually fell into disuse and was eventually replaced by pipes and sprinklers. Hiking trails, roads, and a smoldering landfill would over time be built on the mountainside as Penticton grew, and the benchland would eventually attract architecturally designed wineries and sprawling housing developments. But during my childhood the terraces were covered by an almost unbroken sea of wavering green fruit trees, with occasional grand farmhouses where estates had flourished.

My parents arrived in the Okanagan Valley just as the old world of gentlemen farmers was fading away. Our house was purchased from a retiring orchardist, his skin as brown and tough as tree bark, who was among the last of a generation being pushed out by more mechanized agricultural operations and by the growing demand for housing. With no children willing to take over from him, Mr. Glass sold us the manor, which had been in his family since 1908. The once-great orchard he'd planted was divided among other farmers and eventually would be split again among land speculators who dreamed of sprawling suburbs.

The front yard of the old Glass house was flanked by two huge redwoods, a gateway that towered above the fruit trees and drew in hawks, which perched on the nodding tip-tops, peering down at our chickens. The hens were guarded by a big Barred Rock rooster that attacked any perceived threat—dogs, cats, or little boys—that came near his flock. He was a terror who jumped up to rake my legs with his spurs. Whenever he saw me he charged, and I ran. One day when he attacked, I blindly swung a stick, struck the side of his head, and knocked him cold. When he regained consciousness, he staggered a few steps, eyes rolling, found his balance, looked at me, and ran for the henhouse. After that, whenever he saw me he fled. Later in life I would teach my daughters always to stand up to bullies—it was a lesson I learned from a chicken.

The driveway dipped around our home, which was built on an elevated platform of land surrounded by a low dry-stone wall. It gave the building a stately appearance, as if it commanded the orchards surrounding it. Inside the front door the hallway was finished with richly toned oak wainscoting, and a grand staircase led to upstairs bedrooms wallpapered with red velvet oak leaves on a creamy background. On the ground floor, off the front hall, was a parlor finished in wood, with a large fireplace. Over the mantelpiece was an oil painting in the Scots Romantic style, depicting a noble stag standing on a craggy outcrop.

The house cost $5,000 and it was a dramatic change from the tiny, two-room fruit-picker's cottage we had been renting on the shore of Skaha Lake, a few miles south of Penticton. When we moved into the new house, the children running awestruck through the big, open rooms, we found that Mr. Glass had left behind a collection of oak furniture with brass drawer pulls, carved headboards, and reeded legs. His once-prosperous family had imported the pieces from England when the orchards bloomed with promise. The abandoned furniture, made with old English oak, which glowed honey brown, dated back to the 1800s. "Round the Horn, under sail," was penciled on the bottom of one dresser drawer.

This furniture had crossed the Atlantic from England, and about sixty years later my parents, almost penniless and with all their possessions packed in a few trunks, had followed by ocean liner to Canada's East Coast, and by transcontinental train to Vancouver Island—their first child,

Stephen, in tow, and my mother pregnant with Timothy, their second. Two years after, I was born in Victoria, and a few years later, my younger brothers followed. We lived on the West Coast for several years, in a series of small towns, before moving to Penticton, into the old Glass house, in an old orchard, near a trout stream.

———

TO GET TO PENTICTON CREEK I walked through the neat lines of fruit trees, then cut down a gully, where the chaos of nature regained control. Chokecherries, willows, and cotton-woods grew in a tangle along the stream. I carried my new fishing rod, full of hope. Peering through the bushes I could see the trout hanging in the current where I'd seen them on my last trip, before I tore myself open on the piece of glass.

There were schools of a dozen or more brook trout in each pool. But getting them with a rod wasn't as easy as throwing rocks at them. I began by drifting a bobber downstream, with a worm dangling beneath it, feeding out line until the float reached the school of trout in the pool. Or I tried. Often, however, the plastic bobber was pushed off track by a way-ward current or gust of wind. Sometimes the fish fled before I even made a cast, spooked as I clambered about in, and sometimes fell out of, the bushes. But with each outing I learned to move with greater stealth, and as I studied the fish, I came to see that the brookies took up their positions with deliberation. They weren't chasing things randomly, but placed themselves so the current brought insects and other food to them. With minimal effort they would turn to one side or the other, or tilt up, to take a bug.

This was a revelation. Nature had order. The trick for me was to splice myself into it, to find the thread of current that ran directly to the trout. When I got it right, the float drifted along a seam of water, presenting the worm naturally to a waiting trout, and then the float bobbed as the fish nipped the bait. When the stream made a seemingly natural offering of food to the fish in that way, they could not resist.

I had to wait until the bobber was pulled fully under before I set the hook. If I struck too soon, the fish escaped with a piece of worm in its mouth, not the hook, and the plastic float came skittering back loudly on the surface, scaring the rest of the trout in the school.

Learning to wait until the fish took the entire bait was difficult, but holding my breath helped, and after the first trout was successfully hooked and brought splashing to my feet, I made rapid progress. By the second summer of fishing with a rod I was again bringing home strings of trout, dangling from willow branches like wild fruit, and there was an urge in me to catch more and more fish.

I always wanted another. I had not yet learned temperance. And I had not yet learned how to let trout go, killing all that I caught. I cleaned them beside the stream, leaving their guts for birds, turtles, and snakes. At home I washed the trout in the kitchen sink, trying to make them as beautiful as they were when I first pulled them from the water. But I saw how their slick skin wrinkled, and their colors faded. Death had a pallid look. Green became gray, the vibrant red spots rusted away, and the supple bodies of the trout became stiff. Laid out on the counter they weren't the same vivid creatures I took from the stream. I felt regret, but not enough to question my role; fishing was instinctive and bringing trout home confirmed my skill.

I spent most of my summer days on the creek with my brothers and friends, fishing, swimming, and chasing venomous water moccasins or painted turtles when I couldn't find trout. I fished all up and down the creek, from the stream mouth where the current sank into Okanagan Lake and where I saw carp drifting by like dirigibles around the docks, up to the base of the dam where I cast into the swirling water that seldom yielded fish and that always felt threatening. I knew that behind the dam the lively little creek had formed a lake that was closed to public access. We used to gaze through the chain-link fence and wonder what it would be like to fish in a lake where nobody else fished. But there were regular patrols and we knew we'd get caught if we fished openly.

One day I and my friend Gordy, who shared a love of fishing with me, climbed up the rocks beside the dam and snuck through a hole in the fence that surrounded the drinking water reservoir. There were "No Trespassing" signs posted along the fence, but we were determined to fish Penticton Creek above where it flowed into the lake. Stephen had been there before with one of his adventurous friends, and I had seen on a map a blue thread coming out of the mountains to feed the reservoir. Steve said there was a big pool up there, called Castle Rock, and the stream ran free through a wild forest, out of sight of the water board patrols.

I wanted to go there, to see the stream for myself.

Gordy and I ran down a service road beside the reservoir, found the stream, and began to walk up it. Unlike the lower creek with its concrete spillways, the stream above the reservoir was unspoiled. It rushed through gardens of rocks, creating a choir that echoed off the forest. Deep pools formed on the bends and my heart beat at the thought of what trout they might hold. I marveled at how wild things made their own world, at how everything flourished away from the streets, manicured lawns, and tidy orchards.

We fished and wandered and listened to the birds sing in the forest canopy. And then, on that forbidden stream, in a pool dark as slate, I saw a big trout emerge from under a rock ledge and return to hide.

I stopped breathing for a moment.

Never had I imagined a trout that big could exist. Most of the brookies we caught were ten to twelve inches long, and the largest I'd ever seen was a spectacular eighteen-inch trout that one of the older boys had caught. It weighed about two pounds.

But now, standing in the stream in my runners, my jeans wet to the knees, I was within casting range of an enormous fish that looked to be at least five pounds. I swung the weighted line, let it drop on a patch of water the size of a baseball hat, and saw the worm plunge toward the shadows under the ledge. Nothing stirred, and I knew the worm would need to be presented naturally to fool such a big fish.

I took off the weight. Cast again, softly, feeding out line so the worm drifted slowly, naturally with the current. I was in the seam. The worm tumbled along the edge of the shadows—twisting on the hook—and the trout swam out, turned casually, and took the bait back into hiding.

I tightened the line. Then there was an enormous yank. A shock went up the line, through the rod into my hands and arms.

That fish pulled harder than any fish ever has or ever will.

When it fought, its body roiled the pool. Its flanks shone silver and white in the water. Its red spots flashed. Its gill plates flared when it shook its head. I would not give it line and stood there with the rod bent so hard it seemed about to break. But the line, the hook, and the flimsy rod held. I shouted for help.

Stumbling backward I dragged the brawling trout out of the depths and into the shallows, toward the aluminum net—which Gordy, wide eyed and cursing at the size of the fish, brought running. He lunged and missed, tried again, jamming the net under the writhing fish and lifting. But the net was too small. For a moment the trout hung there, its head out one side, its tail and lower body out the other. None of us moved. Then it thrashed, knocking the net away, throwing the hook and crashing into the water at our feet.

And just like that it was gone, back to the infinite mystery of the depths. The last thing I saw was its enormous tail, trailing a fine skein of bubbles. I stood there, unable to speak, hands shaking, bereft.

"You just lost a trophy," said Gordy. "You coulda had your picture in the newspaper!"

But not now. Nobody wanted a story about a lost fish. I felt dazed, as if I had been spit out by a giant trout, like Mr. Jeremy Fisher.

We snuck back out of the reservoir that afternoon, hiding in the underbrush when a water board truck came down the service road, the engine slowly ticking over, sniffing the air for us. We lay still, our rods beside us, and when the truck was out of sight we ran.

Outside the fence I looked back across the shining reservoir to where the rich vegetation marked the stream. The risk had been worth it. We found the headwaters and a wild trout had redefined the limits of fishing for me. It was possible, I realized that day, to be overpowered by a fish.

At first I was upset by the loss, but eventually I came to realize that everyone should lose a great fish in their lifetime, and if it comes early, so much the better. A big fish like that will haunt you. It will live in your memory. And you will spend a lifetime searching for it, trying to catch it in any water that you can—which is truly a wonderful thing to do.

The spell was cast—and I couldn't pass any water after that without scanning the surface, wondering if there was a big fish hiding there, somewhere in the darkness.

I knew there had to be. I just had to find it.

I CAME TO BELIEVE AS IF by osmosis that fishing was my calling. This was what I did—I searched for the mystery in water, and while other boys were worrying about girls, or getting on the school basketball team, I was thinking about Penticton Creek, about its seasons, about how brook trout behaved, and about how far up the headwaters I might go next time. I didn't know it then, but that stream had become what fly fishers call their "home water"—a place to which they are intimately connected. But then that connection was broken.

"I've got a new job. We'll be leaving Penticton," my father announced one day. We were going to live in a distant, big city, which I knew nothing about. All I knew was that I would have to find a new creek to call home.

ATIM
CREEK

WE LEFT THE OKANAGAN VALLEY when I was ten, taking the antique furniture but leaving the grand old house, the lush orchards, and the magic of Penticton Creek behind.

When we moved, going east across the Rocky Mountains from British Columbia to the flatlands of central Alberta, the change of landscape was disorienting. In our new province there were no mountains for the countryside to lean up against. The land was covered with small, sinewy trees instead of vivid green orchards, and Mill Creek Ravine, near our home in Edmonton, didn't hold a blue trout stream but a dull, sluggish trickle stained with mud. I didn't fish the creek, but I followed it downstream. It ran into a pipe that dumped into the brawling North Saskatchewan River, where it sank without a trace.

The Saskatchewan flowed through the middle of Edmonton, not far from our green stucco house on a suburban street. But it wasn't like any water I'd seen before. In winter it froze. At spring breakup it was a runaway train, rattling and squealing on the corners as cakes of swirling, dirty ice jostled in confusion. In summer the river was so heavy with silt it slid past with a slow sucking sound.

I had no idea how to fish such big, muddy, disturbed water, couldn't imagine what swam in it, and left my rod in the closet, the tackle box closed. It was a missed opportunity, because the river has goldeye, walleye, northern pike, and mountain whitefish, but that was unknown to me then and there was no one to show me the way. Instead of haunting the riverbank, peering into the murky water for fish, I lived a city life—hanging out on street corners, having schoolyard fistfights. Disconnected from nature, without home waters to retreat to, I felt a vexation of spirit I didn't understand. But my mother did, and she must have seen it in her other children too as we struggled to adapt to the change from rural to city life. After a year she was lobbying for a move out of Edmonton. Wanting her five boys closer to nature, she persuaded our father to rent a house in the country. I didn't hear those conversations, but they must have been difficult. In Edmonton he was a short drive from work; a move to the country would mean a long daily commute.

But Mother insisted: the city was no place for her children. She found a farmhouse forty minutes outside Edmonton, adrift in a patchwork of wheat fields, bush lots, and ink-black sloughs. And so we moved, into a white clapboard farmhouse where the nearest neighbor was a mile away, out of sight across rolling grain fields. There were no street-lights on the country roads that divided the land neatly into

640-acre sections, and when darkness descended it was so total the stars spread out in a vast, shining blanket that seemed to float above us, just out of reach.

Our water was brought from the ground by a squeaking hand pump; heat came from a woodstove, and we washed cold in the kitchen sink. The house was next to a ramshackle chicken coop and a weathered red barn filled with hay and mice. A boardwalk went from the kitchen to the outhouse, which was skimmed with ice in winter and lit by a bare light bulb.

It may sound harsh, but it was what we knew and it was good. And the chance to learn from nature was there every day. It was just outside the door.

The house was set on open land, cleared by farmers to make way for crops, but wild forests still clung to the marginal land. Trees were left around fields to break the fierce winds, and the tough, knotty trunks grew defiantly anywhere they could. Surrounding the house were thickets of trembling aspen and elegant birch, trees as white as paper with black scars etched on their bark; runes that might tell the mysteries of the forest if they could be read. The bigger bush lots sometimes covered more than a section of land, which was enough to get lost in for a day, and I soon learned the prairie forest was richer in wild animals than the planted orchards of the Okanagan Valley.

Father worked in the city at the *Edmonton Journal*; Mother ran our house in the country; we ran free in the bush. I could vanish all day, as long as I had a sandwich in my pocket and my dog with me for protection.

The countryside didn't mean much to my father, but the arrangement suited him. His job as a political reporter was consuming and he stayed overnight in the city whenever he worked late, which was often. I could sense the tension when he came home after several nights away and I could see it in my mother's eyes. I was only eleven, but I knew there was something broken and dangerous in the world of adults, something hidden, like a piece of glass in the water. A touch of darkness edged into the innocent joy of my childhood.

But I left those worries behind in the forest, running through the woods and the dappled sunlight, with the wind in the canopy sounding like rushing water. Penticton Creek had shown me the hidden world of trout; now the prairie landscape sheltered me and drew me in, revelatory and riven with wild birds and strange creatures, including flying squirrels that glided from tree to tree like paper airplanes, and porcupines that rattled as they ran.

The woods rang with songs of flycatchers and vireos; grouse thrummed in the underbrush and fierce hawks fell from the sky, breaking the necks of their prey. Along the fencerows pheasants ran, then rose with hard, indignant squawks, their wings thudding. Snowshoe hares scattered in the bush, lippity lip, and much larger white-tailed jack-rabbits raced off across the open prairie, moving so fast they lost their shape and became brown smears of light.

At night from my bedroom window I heard somber great gray owls call across the woods as the Milky Way spiraled above. And once, in moonlight, I looked out to see a Canada lynx drift past on padded feet as big as cushions, as silent as snow falling on snow. It ran atop its own shadow, atop the shadows of the trees, reading the runes as it went.

Exploring, I discovered forest trails where the grass was worn away by generations of snowshoe hares, etching their lives into the earth with small, thumping feet. Following those rabbit runs I always felt as if I was entering a secret world, treading where the hares had leaped, tracing the history of their movements through hedges and into dense willow thickets. I found their forms hidden in the forest, small nests where they rested during the day, coming out to feed at night.

One fall it grew cold but didn't snow. It was a betrayal of the natural timing of the seasons, and the snowshoe hares, whose brown and gray summer coats had been perfect camouflage through the fall, were starkly revealed by the unexpected delay of winter. They turned white and I saw them sitting still in the leafless forest, apparently certain that they were unseen even though they stood out like flags. If I made eye contact, or stalked toward them, they would startle, flashing white as they darted through the underbrush. When it finally did snow they vanished again, white into white, and all I saw were their footprints bounding through the bush, the big hind paws showing where they had pushed off and pointing in the direction of travel.

There were more deeply beaten trails too, made by porcupines that left scuff marks by dragging the tender tips of branches into their burrows. Some of the old porcupine dens were almost big enough for me to crawl into, my head pushing into the darkness, listening for the sounds of one moving below and catching the musty smell of a forest hermit drifting up through the tunnels. Around the porcupine dens I had to watch for dropped quills, as slender and lethal as the tips of darts. A few stuck in my hands and I pulled them out, gripping the shafts with my teeth, the fishhook barbs extracting tiny biopsies of pink flesh.

One trail led to another.

And then I made a great find—a stream of shining dark water cut a path through the willows and across the fields. I missed Penticton, but discovering Atim Creek snaking across the prairie landscape a few miles from our house— and hearing from boys at school that it probably held northern pike—stirred hope. So I dug out my fishing rod, checked the line, tied on a lure, and set it in my closet. Just having it ready made me feel better. I planned to hike to the creek, and fish it, as soon as I could.

———

WE LIVED SEVERAL MILES OUTSIDE the farming town of Spruce Grove, which was then made up of a general store, gas station, school, and a cluster of houses around an Alberta Wheat Pool elevator. Lost in the vast prairie land-scape, huddled in the darkness, the small village asserted its presence every night when the civil defense siren sounded. At 9:00 PM a forlorn, mechanical, wailing sound rose up in the starry sky; it started low, grew in volume, gained alti-tude, then after a few minutes lost its energy and fell into silence, leaving a vacuum that nature soon filled with its own night sounds.

The siren wasn't a warning of danger, but was a reminder by the village council that it was time for all children, espe-cially teenagers, to be home. That was the curfew call, but at school we learned if the alarm sounded at any other time of day or night, it would signal an incoming attack from Russia. In the same droning way they assigned home-work, our teachers told us that in the event of a nuclear strike, we should curl up under our desks to survive the initial shock wave and then hide indoors until the radiation

settled. Nobody said what we should do after that. I imagined clouds of radioactive dust drifting across fields and
bush lots, falling with a soft hiss, like sleet. I wondered
where the snowshoe hares, pheasants, and other animals
would hide.

For me the nightly siren, or rather the noise that rushed
in after it ended, was a call to the wild, a reminder of the
mysteries that lay in the forest near our farmhouse. When
the curfew sounded I opened the back door to listen as
coyotes began to howl in response, their doleful, reverent,
fearful voices intertwining in the night air, a scattered pack
reconnecting. They yelped and yowled and let out long, sonorous calls, voices of affirmation answering what they must
have felt was a great, lost coyote, baying somewhere in the
distance. Standing beside me, her hair bristling, our dog
would gruff and press against my legs, trembling at the wild
yapping just outside the perimeter of the farmyard.

I rarely saw coyotes during the day, except when the dog
would suddenly stop in the stiff-legged, big chested way that
dogs do when bluffing bravery, and I'd look up to see one
ghosting across the stubble fields, or standing on a fencerow,
watching us. They could materialize and vanish like smoke.
There it was, staring balefully across the space between us,
and then there it wasn't.

But the nightly cacophony triggered by the siren made
it clear there were many more out there than what we ever
saw; there were dozens of them within earshot of our farm.
Their yelps were sharp and piercing, so close they sounded
just beyond the cone of yellow cast by the porch light. Whenever I heard that collective howling I gripped the door, ready
to slam it shut, and held my dog back.

The coyotes hunted gophers and hares around the farm, mostly, but would come into the yard to kill chickens or house cats when they got a chance. And I knew if they could they would bait our dog, draw her into the dark forest by pretending to play, and then the pack would tear her apart. All that would be left would be a few tufts of fur and maybe her feet.

———

THE BUSH NEAR OUR HOME was laced with snowshoe hare runs that darted through the forest in an intricate, unfathomable pattern. My brother Tim set traps on trails that intersected with other trails, that tied in to runways and darted into cover. The trick was to guess which of the hundreds of pathways had steady traffic and which were little used byways.

A Cree boy on a neighboring farm had taught him how to weave willow branches together to make little fences that guided hares into leghold traps, which snapped shut on anything that depressed the bait pan. Tim only had a few of those traps, rust brown and stained with blood, but also set snares of supple copper wire that drew tight until it cut into an animal's neck. Of the two ways to die, the leghold was the worst—but not by much.

There is no denying the natural cruelty and efficiency of trapping. Having seen how effective my brother was on his small line in a tiny segment of bush on the vast prairies, I have wondered what the natural world would have been like for me, for my daughters' generation, had millions of hares, beavers, muskrats, lynxes, coyotes, wolverines, minks, and foxes not been stripped from the land for centuries by commercial trapping, the founding industry of the nation. While the fur trade brought commerce to remote places, it also greatly diminished nature. The richness of the land was bled away.

That didn't worry me then. I admired the bush knowledge needed to catch something wild in its own world. And we ate the hares, which were gamey but tender as willow buds. Also, I knew that death was all around in nature and others would deliver it if we didn't. I heard that message in the cry of the hawk, the howl of the coyote, the stalking silence of the passing lynx. I saw it in the bleached bones and blood-stained tufts of fur we found in the forest. We studied the kill sites, trying to determine the predator from the swirl of tracks and to identify the prey from the fragmented remains in the hair-entangled scat.

Sometimes I made the rounds with Tim on his trapline, walking through a pale forest that lay quiet in spinning snow. At thirty below zero our breath was sharp and our feet grew so cold we couldn't feel the ground. We became the snow; ice prickled our nostrils, and every few hours we made a campfire to thaw our numb feet, sitting so close to the flames our boot soles smoked.

When we found hares they were usually dead in the traps, occasionally so fresh their bodies were limp, the fur soft and warm. But often they were frozen and twisted on the ground, a thin wire choking them, a dribble of pink foam turned to ice on their mouths. Death has a look and, as with the trout, there was no beauty in it. I understood that killing was the cost of living off the land, but it was harder to be detached from the death of hares, soft and lovely to touch, than from cold-blooded fish.

And hares, unlike fish, can cry out, uttering a plaintive, high-pitched squealing sound so startling and freighted with pain that once heard it is impossible to forget. I learned to imitate the sound by sucking on the back of my hand, and standing in the bush I could call in foxes, weasels, ravens, and hawks by imitating a rabbit in distress. The sound of a small animal in pain always draws a crowd in the hungry forest.

Sometimes on the trapline the only thing left was a stain of blood in the snow, a flurry of tracks telling a story punctuated by a chunk of fur, or a hare's foot clamped in a trap's jaws, everything else eaten.

"Coyotes," Tim said, studying the tracks. "Stealing from my line."

He once gave me a severed rabbit's foot for good luck, but thinking of the way its owner had died, first caught by the trap then devoured by the predator, I later buried it in the forest, under the snow.

Tim always set the traps. I followed, my bow and a quiver of homemade arrows cut from willow branches always at the ready. I shot at squirrels as they rattled through the pines around us, the arrows with their imperfect shafts usually twisting away from the target to bounce harmlessly off tangles of boughs or stick with a satisfying thunk into a tree trunk. Sometimes a grouse would thunder up off the ground, trailing snow, and an arrow would zoom after it, hopefully following its flight path for a moment before falling harmlessly to earth.

I never killed anything with the bow, except for one hapless porcupine that blundered into an open field and got caught by a little boy who didn't know better. After the porcupine was dead I touched its smooth quills, turned it over carefully, its loose body bristling and shedding barbed spines. I saw its unprotected belly; its hidden vulnerability.

Porcupines hug the ground and I then saw why. Their backs are covered with fearsome quills, but their bellies only have soft hairs for protection. Kneeling next to the limp body I also saw for the first time that porcupines have pleading brown eyes and gentle, grandfatherly faces. I laid my hand on its stomach and felt it growing cold.

It's hard to understand death when you are young; but when you cause it, it grips you, bringing a feeling of weakness, not of strength. That moment would never leave me: the hunter, the innocent prey, the need for forgiveness that couldn't be given.

That day I walked home through the forest, my dog quiet behind me instead of leaping ahead, searching for game. I knew she didn't feel good about the killing either. The animal hadn't been needed for food and the death had been pointless.

But I kept my bow. Going armed in the woods meant I was a hunter who might one day bag a plump grouse or hare for a family dinner, and it made me feel like I belonged in the bush. If you hunt you are joined with the forest, not apart, not just a bystander or a pedestrian traveling through. As a hunter, the woods enter you as much as you enter the woods.

The family dog always came with me. A blonde border collie, she had been found before we moved to Alberta from the Okanagan. The family was on a Sunday drive on Green Mountain Road, near Penticton, to pick watercress in a small stream, when we saw a puppy huddled in the ditch.

"It looks abandoned," said my mother. The boys all clamored to bring the ball of fluff into the car. The lumbering 1950s Plymouth drifted to a slow stop and my father leaned over to look out the window.

"Well, somebody better go get it," he said. I bolted out and carried the puppy back. She was only a few weeks old and my mother kept her alive at first with a baby bottle, feeding her warm milk from our goat.

She grew into a hunting dog in Spruce Grove, where she learned to chase game birds out of the long grass and to find squirrels in the forest canopy. She would bark up a tree until a squirrel left its hiding place in irritation and ran out on a branch to chatter down at the bothersome dog, giving me a shot. I would always miss with my arrows, but close was thrilling enough, maybe better.

She hunted with me in the forest and hiked with me down the dirt road that ran past our house and disappeared north, straight over the horizon. Along the way the range road crossed Atim Creek, languid dark water that twisted slowly through the bush, elbowing into willow thickets on its way to Atim Lake, Big Lake, and the Sturgeon River. The creek snaked under root wads, trickled over beaver dams, and in the spring overflowed into farm ditches, where pike hunted for ducklings and mice in the flooded grass. It was a long way from the sparkling trout stream I was imprinted on. But there was a wildness to it I liked, untamed, unruly nature, and the fish sometimes showed themselves in the shallows.

A pike's camouflaged, bluish-green skin is almost invisible against weeds, but its dark shadow gives it away, and then, if you stare hard enough, its gold, bean-shaped spots come into focus and its form takes shape. Sometimes all I would see was a tail, wavering in the current, the rest of the fish's body buried in weeds: a hunter, hidden.

Northern pike are long and narrow, with dark backs and mottled dorsal fins set well back on their bodies, near the tail. They have a duck-billed snout, large canine teeth, and big jaws that snap shut like a leghold trap. Unlike a trout, which is designed to tilt up to take small dry flies from the surface, a pike is built to be launched; it is a spear waiting to be thrown. It lies in hiding, then jolts its prey with a piston strike. It is all tooth and muscle and bone. When it kills a fish too big to swallow, it chews until it breaks its victim in half, leaving shredded flesh and silver scales spinning in the water. It will take a mouse or duckling from the surface with a terrible ripping sound, then the water will go silent as the fish sinks to the bottom to digest its prey. Relentlessly hungry and aggressive, pike will attack almost anything: there have been stories of them taking muskrats, or small dogs, or even slashing at the noses of drinking cattle.

I fished the stream at first with little trout spinners and took some juvenile fish, but the big pike, the wolves of the water, eluded me.

"Pike want a mouthful," an old man who rented rowboats at Atim Lake told me when Tim and I wandered onto his dock one summer afternoon, looking for a place to fish.

A small spinner dangled from my rod and he shook his head in disapproval. His face and boots, creased and weathered brown, seemed made from the same cut of old leather. Stooped, too old to farm anymore, he sat on a wooden chair on the dock, with stained fingers, a tin of tobacco and Zig-Zag cigarette rolling papers in his lap, waiting for fishermen to drive in from the city. He opened an old metal tackle box and there, bright as Christmas decorations, were trays of spoons and plugs, bitten, chewed, and chipped by the fish he'd caught. He showed me his prized Rapalas, minnow imitations carved from balsa wood with hooks in place of pectoral fins, and a collection of spoons—white with red stripes, yellow with red or black diamonds—and a Cisco Kid Topper lure with a red head, white body, and spinner blades fore and aft that churned the water.

He looked at my little rod and asked if I had any money to rent a boat.

"No sir."

"Did you pass school this year?"

"Yes sir."

"Then you can have a boat for free as a reward."

He loaned me a Red Devil spoon too—red and white stripes on the front, silver on the back—and told me to troll it along the weed beds. He waggled his hand to show me how it should flutter in the water.

"But leave your dog on the dock," he said. "Big pike and a dog in the boat is not a good mix."

So off we set, Tim rowing. Halfway around the lake we looked back and saw the dog, swimming behind us, not far from where the Red Devil was wobbling under the surface. We pulled her in, skinny with wet fur and shaking off on us, then we finished the circumnavigation without a bite and I returned the spoon with thanks. The old man was surprised I hadn't caught any pike.

"Probably scared by the dog," he said. "Don't like the smell of her in the water maybe."

A small dog, he said, would not have made it around the lake. "Seen a pup pulled under by a pike once," he said. "Gone. Just like that."

And as I left: "Try the crick. Sometimes big pike go up in there. But get some proper spoons."

At the gas station in Spruce Grove I bought a Red Devil and a yellow-and-red Len Thompson Five of Diamonds, both lures I had seen in the old man's tackle box. They cost fifty-five cents each and were stapled to cards that had fishing hints printed on them. Basically the advice was: just add water and cast the spoon.

I couldn't afford a Rapala, which sold for nearly two dollars, but soon learned I didn't need one. It turned out the Red Devil and Five of Diamonds are two of the best pike lures ever invented. Those, and a few wire leaders to keep the pike from cutting the line with their teeth, were all I needed. The spoons rattled in the air when I cast them, landing with a meaty plop, and the fish in Atim Creek came after them, not with the dainty plucking approach of trout taking a worm, but with lunging, hungry strikes that ripped the water.

The pike were typically two feet long; they had glaring, defiant eyes and sharp teeth that left scars on the painted lures. And the more scarred and battered a lure became, the better it seemed to work. It was as if the pike could see the tooth marks left by other fish and it enraged them.

As I fished the creek that summer I learned that the bigger pike often lay deep under overhanging willows, buried in the roots. Sometimes they were hiding in weeds next to the bank and if I startled them, I would see a swirl of water as they darted for deeper water. It was hard to tell their size from the splash, but some of them seemed bigger than muskrats.

Beside a beaver dam on the creek one day I found what looked like the skull of a dog.

"That's a northern pike," said Tim, pulling out of the drying mud a string of vertebrae stitched together by desiccated skin and cartilage. It looked like the remains of a giant snake.

"I bet it came up here to spawn, then got trapped when the water dropped," he said.

Spread wide, the jaws of the pike's skull could take in my whole face. I touched the teeth, still sharp as needle points. I fished with a new wariness after that, aware that hidden in the weeds, sheltering under the tangled deadfalls, there might be not only a great fish, but a dangerous fish.

One day my Red Devil disappeared in a bucket-sized swirl of water; there was heavy resistance and I wrestled in a ten-pound pike. A big hunter up from the lake, it thrashed the water as I dragged it ashore. Its tail touched the ground as I walked home from Atim Creek, whose waters I had come to love and understand.

IN THE FOREST I BEGAN to collect bird eggs, watching hawks, flickers, kingbirds, and magpies until I learned where they nested. To find a nest I traced the flight of a bird across the sky, and when it vanished in the forest, I fixed its last known location. Then I went to the spot, waited until it reappeared, and did the same thing again, slowly drawing closer. It was like exploring a maze or unraveling a fantastical wire sculpture by picking a single strand and tracing it back to where it began. Sometimes it took days to find a nest. And then I had to climb a tree and reach blind into a cavity, not knowing what I'd find, while birds tried to protect their nests by diving at my head.

An American kestrel came so close I felt her brush my face. An eastern kingbird struck the back of my head with its knuckled toes. A hard rap that was more startling than painful. With a shock I realized that not only could I enter her world, but she could come into mine too.

The kingbird's nest was not hidden in the trees but perched under the overhang of a school friend's barn roof. When I climbed to the roof ridge and looked down I saw a perfect oval of grass, woven together with strips of bark, bits of paper, and a strand of bright-orange baling twine. Nestled inside were four creamy brown eggs with dark, abstract splotches daubed on the shell.

Beyond the nest, which I could just reach with my outstretched fingertips, was a thirty-foot drop to the ground. I knew if I thought of falling, I would fall, so I concentrated on the nest as the birds dove at my head. I sat up, put one egg in my shirt pocket, and shinnied back down the spine of the barn roof, the egg bumping softly against my breast, the kingbirds swooping around me, emitting buzzing, electrical calls of alarm, their beaks snapping.

I would only take an egg if there were four or more in a nest. I found many nests with just two eggs and broken shells, a sign they had already been raided by crows or squirrels. My competitors were fierce and unrelenting.

I pricked the collected eggs at both ends with a needle, blew out the murky yellow contents, and arranged the empty shells, dry and light, in a Black Magic chocolate box my mother had left over from Christmas. The eggs were blue or green or white or caramel and spotted with brushstrokes of brown or smoky gray. When the box was full, the eggs nestled together like chocolate truffles, and it felt like I had completed a set.

By then a dozen species had been traced through the sky. I could identify the birds that laid those eggs by their plumage, their flight patterns, nest types, and calls. I knew how they fit into the landscape. It was hard information to gain, but like learning to read the water in Penticton Creek and figuring out where the big pike lay hidden in Atim Creek, it felt important.

As I studied the flight paths I began to understand the deepest secrets of the forest. The movement of birds wasn't random, but calibrated. Like fish they seemed to be pieces fitted into a complex puzzle, an intricate, ancient web of which I had become a part.

I noticed birds often sat on the same branches, at the same time of day. A bird carrying grass or digging up mud was building a nest. A bird that caught insects but didn't eat them, collecting a bristling beak full, was going to feed its young. Often the parent birds would perch, alert for predators, before making a final dash to a hidden nest. I began to recognize the pose and would watch for the bird to make that last, revealing flight to its nest. Then I saw it: a small cavity drilled in a tree trunk or a camouflaged nest wedged into branches. The nests were woven from slender wheatgrass, fescue, sticks, and mud; they were lined with down or silky thistle fluff.

Coming back from the creek my dog found a duck's nest knitted into a mound of grass in a dusty roadside ditch far from water. I didn't know ducks would often nest in dry places to avoid predators and then, after the hatch was complete, they would lead their ducklings across country to water. Worried the nest had been built in a bad place, just a few steps from where farm trucks rumbled past, and then abandoned by a feckless mother, my brother and I collected all seven of the bluish-green eggs. We carried them home in our baseball hats and put them in the chicken coop under a heat lamp. They hatched into yellow puffballs. They were mallards, and we raised them with the leghorn chickens. As ducklings they followed us around the farmyard, came running to feed from our hands, and sat in our laps. They learned to swim in the horse trough, circling like water beetles.

That fall, after the ducks developed flight feathers on their awkward wings, we put them in a cardboard box and let them go at a slough where thousands of waterfowl were staging for migration. When the box was opened they saw flocks of wild mallards dabbling in the weeds. These were the first ducks they had ever seen other than themselves, but they rushed to join them, instincts intact.

A few weeks later I saw the ducks rising up in great clouds, like smoke over the prairies, circling, then forming into wedges, great formations of waterfowl streaming south. Somewhere lost among them were the mallards we had raised. But as I turned for home with my dog I wondered if they would safely make the flight south, or if they would get shot, waddling up to a hunter, looking for a handful of feed.

———

THE DOG WAS A CONSTANT in my life. She slept on my bed at night and sat at my feet under the dining room table. She was waiting by the gate when I sprang from the doors of the big yellow school bus and raced down the driveway, with her bounding after me, barking and joyous.

My mother named her Flossie, because she was covered with soft fluff like a duckling when we first found her. The name was fine when we were little boys and she was a puppy. But the fuzz shed. By the time we were living on the Alberta farm, I was almost a teenager and it was not a name I wanted to tell my friends, most of whom lived on farms and saw dogs only as work animals, not pets. So I mostly just called her "Hey, girl," and she came on the run, judging the urgency of the call by the inflection of my voice.

Looking at family photos years later with my brothers I noted they all referred to her as "their dog," and I would think, "Hey, wait a minute, she was *my* dog." But family dogs are like that, giving their affection freely to whoever is there, bonding and ready for any adventure with anyone.

Of all of us, however, I'm the only one who tried to kill her.

The coyotes that raided Tim's rabbit snares, ate our chickens, and were prime suspects in the disappearance of our house cats were pressing in around the farm. I could hear them howling at night, not far away in the forest, and I knew they were coming into the yard. So I cut a length of heavy wire long enough for a snare and, with Flossie at my side, searched for coyote tracks in the bush nearby.

On a rabbit run that wove through a grove of trees near our house I found some prints—oblong, wiry, and determined, not soft and pampered like a dog's. I set a snare at just the right height so a snowshoe hare would pass under it, but the noose would slip over the head of a running coyote, jerking tight on its neck. I imagined finding a coyote strangled and proudly carrying it home draped over my shoulder: Peter and the Wolf.

"The cat killer is dead," I would say.

That night my brothers and I played touch football under the yard lights, running pass patterns with our breath billowing, our bodies hot in the cold air, skittish as colts.

The dog didn't join the game, yapping after the ball carrier as she usually did. I heard her howling in the bush a few times. Chasing hares, I thought. But then running to catch a pass I forgot her. When the curfew siren sounded I heard the coyotes howling and we were called in for bed.

The next morning at breakfast my mother asked if anyone had seen Flossie.

"She didn't come in last night," she said. "That's not like her. I'm worried."

I felt my gut tighten.

I ran from the house into the gray light of the forest at dawn, found the hare trail I'd set the snare on, and raced along the path, jumping deadfalls, stumbling, getting up, running hard, sweating, heart hammering.

When I found the dog she was snared, lying still, the wire tight around her neck. I stopped and stared across the clearing in the wood, feeling like when I shot the porcupine and saw the stupid, irreversible stillness of death.

Then the dog wagged her tail, one weak thump.

I crossed to her, felt warmth and breathing. Her head moved, trying to lift up, then fell back, eyes rolling white. She lay still and waited for me to release the wire.

The dog was so smart that when she felt the noose tighten she stopped pulling. A coyote would have thrashed in panic and bit its own tongue until it choked to death. But she lay there all night, unmoving, waiting for me, listening to the coyotes hunting in the woods nearby.

I tore my fingers working the thin wire off. She was bruised, a purple welt circling her neck under the fur, but not sliced open. I pulled the snare from where it was anchored to an alder branch and saw the bark cut from the tension of the wire, the cambium layer slick as a skinned hare. That could have easily been her neck, I thought; if she'd pulled a little harder, she'd have died.

I carried Flossie home through the forest, putting her down at the edge of the yard so she could run the rest of the way. I never told my mother what happened, hollowly accepted praise for finding the lost dog.

I silently swore I would never set a snare or try to trap a coyote again. I had seen how they would die, alone in the forest.

———

MY MOTHER HAD SUCH FAITH in Flossie's power to protect me that she let me vanish into the woods all day, and that summer we fished together along Atim Creek, ranging upstream and down, catching long, toothy pike. I learned how to cut fillets off the fish to avoid most of the bones, and my mother cooked the white flesh in butter. Exploring the forest had been a revelation, but finding a fishing stream at the heart of it all made me feel grounded, complete.

Then the landlord turned us out of the farmhouse near Spruce Grove, and just like that, we had to pack up and move, away from the wild bush lots and away from Atim Creek, where the pike lurked in the weeds. I had to start over. And I couldn't find any streams near the new house outside Stony Plain, just a few murky sloughs with muskrats.

In Stony Plain we lived beside the Yellowhead Highway, in a small, poorly heated house where hoarfrost formed on the inside of the windows through the long winter. But it was to be a temporary home. For several months my mother raised her boys alone there, after my father took a job in British Columbia, with the *Victoria Daily Times*, one of two competing newspapers in the provincial capital. The plan was for us to stay in Stony Plain until the school year ended, but that changed suddenly after remittance men came to repossess our furniture because of unpaid bills. My mother stood in the kitchen, pulling her children close, as men carried out the couch, the armchair, the television.

"Well, less for us to pack," she said.

Soon after that we moved back to British Columbia. During the drive west we camped in the Rockies, and when I awoke that first morning in the mountains I could hear a river, far away. I felt drawn outside by some compelling force. I pulled back the door flap and saw a wolf near the tent. We stared in silence at each other, then it turned and walked away. I went out while my family slept and stood in the cold morning, in the silent, slumbering campground. And the wolf had vanished. Later that morning we all tumbled into the car and continued our journey. I remember looking out the back window at the great wall of mountains, behind which, far away, the Alberta grasslands lay hidden.

Somehow in the move the Black Magic box, filled with bird eggs, had been forgotten, the secrets of a prairie forest lost. I would never see Atim Creek again; I would never again cast a Five of Diamonds into that black water, hoping for a giant pike. Another home stream abandoned. But I kept my tackle box in the car with me. I wasn't going to lose that. And I thought hopefully of the mysterious waters that lay ahead.

THE
MASTER

I HAD BEGUN TO CALIBRATE my life in relation to my access to water. I had come to love the bush lots and murky pike waters of Alberta, but I looked forward to returning to British Columbia because it would put me near salmon and trout on the West Coast. Looking at a map I saw Victoria was surrounded by the ocean on three sides, and that lakes were scattered around the city, which filled me with hope. My brothers and I would have to adjust to a new home and new schools and make new friends, but instead of worrying about that, I was anticipating the new places I might fish.

Knowing this, my dad gave me a copy of *The Fresh-water Fishes of British Columbia, Handbook No. 5,* by G. Clifford Carl and W. A. Clemens, with black-and-white illustrations by Frank L. Beebe. Published by the BC Provincial Museum in 1948, it contains scientific descriptions of sixty-three species, including five kinds of salmon and nine types of trout and char. There are several color illustrations by E. B. S. Logier (who inexplicably is not credited in the paperback edition), of Kamloops trout, steelhead, cutthroat, and

Dolly Varden—fish as beautiful as exotic birds. Once I had seen Logier's paintings of those fish I knew I had to somehow catch them, to hold them in my hands.

We moved into a house just a few blocks from the ocean, on the outskirts of Victoria, and I soon had new fishing equipment. I upgraded from a simple bait-casting outfit to a Shakespeare Wondercast push-button reel that looked like a small spaceship, a reentry capsule. It was fitted perfectly on a short, sturdy fiberglass rod, and with it I could cast spoons and spinners great distances. When I pushed a button on the back of the reel it lifted a hidden spool, releasing the line, which flowed out with a swishing sound when I cast. Far out on the water I would see the lure drop with a small splash. The reel wound the line back through a tiny opening in an outer cone, wrapping the coils neatly inside the covering. It was delightful and easy to use, but limited in how much line it held, and I soon learned the reel couldn't handle big fish.

Casting for trout in a coastal stream one day I hooked my first salmon, a heavy, solid weight that stopped my spinner deep in the water and held it. It hesitated a moment, deciding what to do, its presence throbbing up the line. Then it raced out of the pool, went through the rapids below, and my little reel began to whine and grind as the gears tried to keep up. But the fish was running too fast. There was a clunking sound as the power of the fish overcame the ability of the mechanism to respond. The reel stopped releasing line, and the salmon, with one last, violent pull, broke off.

After that I got an elegant Garcia Mitchell open-face reel, which operated with a soft whirring sound. Unlike the push-button reel, the Garcia Mitchell had an exposed spool to hold the line. A metal arm clicked open to let line come off in rapidly released coils. On the retrieve, the arm snapped back over the spool, so the line could be wound in. It had silky gears, and when a fish dashed away, the reel smoothly released line at a steady tension. The resistance caused by the gears is known as a reel's drag, and a good drag mechanism will slowly wear a fish down.

Back at the pool where my Wondercast reel had been destroyed I hooked another salmon and this time was able to land it. It was a five-pound coho, with a greenish-blue back, sides the color of polished steel, and amazing golden eyes with black orbs. I could see the ocean in those eyes, the shimmering Pacific seamounts, the dark Aleutian Trench.

With the new reel I soon mastered the art of spin casting, flipping spoons for salmon in the creeks outside Victoria, wobbling plugs past weed beds in lakes for bass, and drifting small spinners through shafts of green light in estuaries to catch sea-run cutthroat trout.

Without any strategy I had been passing through stages of enlightenment in fishing. I advanced from catching trout barehanded, to drifting bait for small fish, to taking rapacious pike on heavy spoons cast with a simple level wind reel, to throwing delicate spinners for trout with a small push-button reel, and finally to learning how to control big Pacific salmon as they ripped line from my open-face spinning reel.

Fishing with my hands had taken an animalistic instinct, but it required no understanding of fish other than that they would flee, and hide when frightened. That is as basic as it gets: throw a rock and trap scared fish in a hole.

Fishing with bait wasn't much beyond that. An angler can go to sleep with a worm sitting on the bottom and still catch fish. Just plunk and wait. A fish comes along, smells the bait, tastes it with a tentative nibble, then swallows it whole and swims away, lethally hooking itself.

A spin caster doesn't need to read the water because a heavy lure sinks quickly, cutting through the currents to probe the depths. And spin casters don't need to know what fish are eating. Lures wobble like injured minnows, and are so enticing that fish strike reactively, even when they aren't hungry.

With each advancement in technology I caught more fish and bigger fish. But I now found myself wanting something more, not just greater skill, but something deeper. I wanted a stronger connection with the natural world. Perhaps because I had moved so much with my family, each time breaking my connection to friends and the water I loved, I felt a sense of detachment, of loss. I wanted a greater sense of belonging— not to a community or school, things which I had learned were ephemeral, but to nature itself, which was indelible. And I had begun to feel that with spin fishing—despite the success I was having catching fish—the connection it gave me to the water was limited, constrained, muted. It was like I was outside a church listening to voices somewhere within. I wanted to go inside, to hear more clearly, to feel nature more fully. And that led me to the next stage.

I saw that with fly fishing I would have to concentrate harder than I ever had before. I would have to be more finely attuned to everything around me. I would have to walk purposefully along the riverbank, stopping the way a blue heron does to study the surface. I would have to become part of what was happening, like a hunter in a forest. Handicapped with the most rudimentary equipment—a simple reel, a long slender rod, a tiny fly that weighed nothing—I would have to do more than just read the surface of the water. I would have to understand the subsurface currents and the feeding behavior of the trout as well.

Fly fishing, I soon understood, was like entering a library. It would tell me stories I'd never heard before. It would bring me deeper into nature and bind me to home waters more deeply than anything ever had.

———

I FIRST LEARNED OF FLY FISHING through popular outdoor magazines, like *Field & Stream*. I was intrigued by the idea of using tiny insect imitations to catch trout, and my imagination was captured by the artistic renderings of big fish leaping high above the water. But my education really began when I stumbled on Roderick Haig-Brown's books on fly fishing one cold, wet winter day while poking through the stacks in the Victoria Public Library. It was then housed in the Carnegie Building, a stately sandstone edifice built in 1904 with an arched portico and stained glass windows that spilled pools of light inside. In those silent rooms literature sat heavy on the shelves, and amid such weighty books I was surprised to find a fishing section. Until then I had thought fishing was regarded by most people as a frivolous pursuit, a simple pastime, and that I had been unusual in revering it. Now I discovered fishing—and fly fishing in particular—had a rich history and a global community of literate anglers who felt as deeply about it as I did.

Volumes had been written about the art and craft of sport fishing. There were books on the history of angling, on knots, on how to read the water, on bass fishing, swordfish fishing, shark and salmon fishing, and whole encyclopedias on artificial flies and how to tie them. Among this trove was a series of Haig-Brown's books about fly fishing, mostly set on the rivers of Vancouver Island, where I lived. He wrote so evocatively and intelligently about fishing and nature that I soon came to think of him as the Master.

Haig-Brown, a dignified, pipe-smoking man who sometimes wore a jaunty trilby while fishing, was alive then and at the height of his fame as a British Columbia writer. He was often quoted in the media, not just for his eloquent writing but also because of his outspoken views on conservation. Haig-Brown campaigned against dams, against profligate logging, against mines that polluted watersheds, and he was critical of the provincial government for allowing widespread environmental destruction. He saw the natural world being eroded through greed and ignorance, and he feared the next generation would not know the wild forests and rivers he knew, would not know the steelhead, trout, and salmon fishing he knew. For the first time I began to think deeply about those issues and to see that the natural world I cherished was under constant threat.

Later, when I was attending the University of Victoria, where he was chancellor in the early 1970s, I heard him speak. I remember sitting quietly at the back of the lecture hall, impressed by his graceful demeanor. He was a great literary figure in British Columbia then and I was a humble student, too intimidated to approach and ask him about fly fishing. A few years after that, in 1976, Haig-Brown died suddenly at his house on the banks of the Campbell River. He was sixty-eight. I like to think that the last thing he heard was the sound of water moving over a bed of ancient stones; his home river, flowing toward something greater.

HAIG-BROWN, A POWERFUL WITNESS TO the diminishment of nature, helped form my environmental views, but
more particularly he drew me into the world of fly fishing,
which shaped my life and later helped shape the lives of
my daughters. I remember taking his books off the shelf
at the library and sitting cross-legged between the stacks,
Fisherman's Spring open in my hands, *Fisherman's Summer*,
Fisherman's Winter, and *A River Never Sleeps* on the floor
beside me. His book *A Primer of Fly-Fishing* became my key
source on the technical aspects of the sport. American artist
Louis Darling illustrated those books with black-and-white
woodcuts so real you can almost feel the rod bending, feel
the weight of the fish pulling underwater. I checked out as
many of the books as the librarian would let me take, and
went back for the rest later.

I was fourteen, poring through Haig-Brown's books at
night in my room when I should have been studying French
or math. Through those books I escaped to the river, wading
in fast water, casting for steelhead and salmon. And for the
first time I came to appreciate that fly fishing is more than
just a hobby; I began to realize that it is a spiritual apprehension, central to the lives of its followers. I knew I had to learn
how to fly fish if I was to join that community, if I was to fish
in a way that honored the water and the fish.

You either have this in your soul or you do not. It is not
taught, but is awakened. And once aroused, it became a for-
mative force in my life. My school friends wanted to grow up
to become rock stars or professional athletes or cops. But as
a teenager I dreamed about becoming like the masters of the
fly rod depicted in Haig-Brown's books. I wanted to join that

brotherhood, to wade deep for steelhead. I wanted to have home waters where I knew the movement of the fish within the movement of the seasons.

———

IN VICTORIA WE LIVED ON the edge of town, where housing developments were just starting to devour agricultural land. Our neighbor was a hay farmer who paid me to haul heavy bales into his barn, chaff sticking to my sweat, the binding rope cutting into my hands. Our home was surrounded by a grove of apple trees and daffodil fields, beyond which lay open pastureland and woodlots. But cul-de-sacs were starting to fragment the pastoral landscape, and soon bungalows and ranchers would engulf it all. The hayfield would become a football stadium, the orchard a housing complex; the pasture where wild pheasants and rabbits ran would become a private tennis club. Outside my window I began to see that development is a tide that never stops rising.

From our house it took an hour to bike through what was then still mostly rural countryside to Elk Lake, where schools of sparkling sunfish or solitary bass could be found lurking under lily pads. But often I fished closer to home, on a rocky point I could walk to where I could cast into the sea for cod and dogfish. They were big, strong fish, but I found I could only catch them on chunks of herring, left sitting on the bottom. That put me where I didn't want to be—back to bait fishing.

Whenever I could convince my dad, he would drive me to one of the local trout lakes, where I could cast small spinners. If I was lucky, we'd make a forty-five-minute trip to Sooke, where trout and salmon streams run into the sea.

My father didn't fish then, but one of his colleagues at the *Victoria Daily Times*, columnist Arthur Mayse, was a devout fly fisher, and he heard about my interest in Haig-Brown. He told my dad to take me to Muir Creek, which held sea-run cutthroat trout.

———

MUIR CREEK RUNS OUT OF a rainforest on the southwest coast of Vancouver Island, near Sooke. It was a rustic logging town then but soon would begin growing relentlessly in the crazy, developer-driven way that so many small West Coast towns have done. Then, forestry operations were just beginning to strip the watersheds, and the Sooke mountains were still covered with thick forests. But slowly, methodically, they were clearcut, as a destructive wave of logging swept over the landscape.

On every visit I would see piles of timber dumped in the booming yard near the mouth of Muir Creek. Logs were stacked in towers and the ground was paved with sludge and chaff. Heavy, grinding machines known as feller bunchers and grapple skidders churned between the stacks of trees, or memories of trees, limbless trunks waiting to be transported to a mill. It was a dead forest, habitat only for machines.

Down the logging road that crossed the highway next to the bridge, lumbering trucks came wheezing. Clattering giants, they rolled into the sorting yard, dropped their loads, the sectioned trunks of great, old trees, and returned to the mountain for more. They were flaying the forest, draining the land of life. The highway crossing was marked with mud and shards of bark. Even a hard rain did not wash the stain away.

On every visit to Muir Creek I looked up at the hillsides and saw how the scabrous clearcuts were spreading over the green landscape. I was young, but I knew then that what I was seeing was wrong. They were destroying the forest, and I realized I was witnessing the desecration of nature Haig-Brown was warning about.

"It's what makes the economy go," said my father, expressing the practicality his generation (and later mine) used to justify so many things. Salmon runs were overfished, rivers dammed, whole mountains stripped of their forests, gas and oil fields fracked—because it was good for the economy. The environmental and spiritual loss caused by all that industrial activity was never measured, but those who fished saw it, felt it, slipping away around them.

———

SOMETIMES WHEN I WAS ON Muir Creek, waiting for a rising tide to bring schools of cutthroat prowling in from the ocean, I would see a fly fisher working the estuary, casting gracefully. I watched from a distance, too timid to approach but studying their movements. I realized my spinning rod had to be replaced, because it would not allow me to enter that world, to fish the way Haig-Brown did. But I didn't have enough money to buy a fly rod and wouldn't until the summer hay harvest. So I watched and grew restless.

For a period one spring my father developed a deeper interest in my passion. Instead of reluctantly giving in to my pestering to take me out, he began offering to take me fishing on the upcoming weekend. He'd set a date and a time for departure. Perhaps in making this effort he was trying to hold on to something, or to make amends for the childhood that had vanished so quickly while he was busy working. Or maybe those trips were just a way to escape spending time with my mother at home, where the tension was growing between them. Whatever the reason, I was so happy to have a fishing trip on my calendar that I would spend the week looking at maps, and because he usually came home from work long after I was in bed, I would leave notes for him about where I thought promising water lay.

When the weekend came we'd go out in the morning, and when the car stopped I would grab my rod and dash off, scrambling along wooded banks. He'd sit in the car reading a book, patient and inscrutable. It wasn't until later I realized his relationship with my mother was ending. We didn't talk of it then, of his fears (if he had any) of leaving his family, of everything we'd known together coming undone. He said nothing of having an interest in another woman. All of that remained hidden. When I think back now of him waiting in the car, I see him as a man turning the blank pages of a book, reading a story written in an invisible ink that only he could see.

Before I ran off to fish he told me when to be back. I usually had two hours. I was always punctual; timing my return to the minute. My father would look at his silver wristwatch, nod, and smile, the contract fulfilled as agreed.

"Catch any?" he would always ask, and sometimes I would hold up a few bass or trout, which I had gutted on the water. I would wash them again later in the kitchen sink, to give my mother a catch clean of blood.

IN AUGUST, ON MY SIXTEENTH BIRTHDAY, I got a fly rod from my parents, and a few days later my father drove my twelve-year-old brother Jon and me out to Muir Creek, where we planned to stay the night. Art Mayse had told him the stream would be a good place to try fishing that month.

"He said the trout are near the mouth in the summer and then move up when the salmon come in to spawn," said Dad, passing on the tip.

I'd caught sea-run cutthroat in Muir Creek by spin casting before. So I knew where the fish sometimes lay, along wooden pylons that lined one bank. I knew the fish came in with the tide, settled in near the pylons, and darted out to chase bait fish. Such knowledge is hard to gain; it is collected, like the trail to bird nests, a bit at a time, by observation. Eventually the pieces form a pattern, and then you see things in nature that others don't, like where birds hide their eggs or where trout rest unseen.

Despite the logging in the hills above us, the stream ran mostly clear in those days; the gravel bars were free of sediment and the sea-run trout came in from the ocean with every rising tide. Sometimes I would see a school of them, their backs breaking the slick surface, creating swirls of bright water. And I would wait, trying to stay calm as they came closer, waiting until the fish were within casting range.

I awoke in the back of my dad's sky-blue Ford Falcon station wagon, my brother Jon sleeping beside me, my dad under a blanket in the front seat. The sun wasn't up yet, and gray light infused the forest. I slipped out of the car, intent on experiencing this moment alone. I wanted the water to myself, to be unhurried in the pursuit not just of trout, but of something bigger—grace, I suppose. I took the fly rod I'd been given and went down into the morning mist rising along the stream.

I headed for the pylons where I knew cutthroat would be holding. For the first time I would try to catch one on a fly. But I also had to learn how to cast.

I knew the basic concept of casting from watching others on the water and from reading every book I could find. Within a few weeks of getting a fly rod I had learned how to shoot line, how to pluck my fly silently from the surface, how to hook the cast to the left or right by turning the rod and accelerating or stopping the line abruptly.

But that morning my casting was awkward and sloppy. It was disjointed, blundering, and potentially dangerous. I slapped the water with my line, hooked willow branches behind me, and hit myself in the back of the head with the fly. *Thwack.*

Finally, in desperation, I tried roll casting, a simple maneuver I'd read about, studying illustrations that showed how the rod is raised slowly then snapped down, so the line rolls up off the water and jumps forward. Roll casting is a mandatory first step for beginners; it is how you initially control your line, and I had been foolish and vain not to start with it.

After a few awkward attempts I soon was able to roll the fly out almost far enough to reach the water where the trout held. I had only a few flies, one a small, bedraggled streamer that by luck was the shape, size, and color of a salmon fry. I waded waist-deep in my blue jeans, shivering in the early coolness as the waterline crept up my body, runners slipping on the slick stones beneath my feet, and got my cast to where I wanted it, close to the pylons. I watched the fly sink into shadows, and when I pulled it back into the light, a pair of cutthroat materialized behind it. Just like that. Suspended in water they glided together, one just slightly deeper and behind the other. They were big fish and I held my breath, felt my body tense. Then one gave a few faster tail beats and darted ahead of the other to engulf the fly.

I lifted the rod, felt it bend deep against the fish, and heard the line hiss as it cut tight across the surface, following the dashing trout. Then the fish jumped, coming up high and splooshing down with a sound that echoed off the bridge in the morning stillness.

I was alone on the stream, at dawn. The only noise was the splashing fish and the metallic rattle of the drag on my reel as the trout pulled out line and I wound it back. That scene is as sharp in my memory now as a Louis Darling woodcut. I see a fly fisher in silhouette, arms up, rod bent, a fish suspended in the air after jumping clear of the surface, leaving a whorl in the water. It was as if I had stepped into *Fisherman's Summer* and I almost expected to look up and find Haig-Brown watching from the bridge as the fish leaped across the page.

Unsure how to land that fish on such a long, slender rod I simply backed up, dragging the fish until it was out of the water, flopping on the gravel bar. I put down my rod and ran forward to catch the cutthroat in my hands. It was heavily spotted, silver and black and green. I pinned it in the rocks, afraid the first trout I had taken on a fly might get away, like the big fish I'd lost on Penticton Creek. I killed the cutthroat with a piece of driftwood, striking it on the head as I had learned to do from watching other fishers. It shuddered and lay still. When I looked up, another fish swirled in the creek, and I stumbled back into the water with my fly rod raised like a talisman.

Later that morning, with the sun fully up, my brother Jon wandered down. "Anything?" he called, rubbing his eyes to wake up. I gestured to the trout on the bank. He whistled, went back to the car to get his spinning rod, and began to fish near me, casting with ease. He hooked and lost a few trout, then landed a pair while our father stood on the bank, cheering whenever one of us brought a fish to shore.

That day I took a dozen cutthroat trout, all about eighteen inches in length. Most I had caught at first light, fishing alone, relishing the solitude of it all, which made the whole experience more intense, and I was glad that no one had been there to watch my early ineptitude with the fly rod. I still dream of those fish, the dark-green backs, the inky star-shaped spots splashed across their sides, the vivid red stripes under their jaws, and the golden-silver sheen. They looked as if they were made from polished amber and confirmed the beauty of fly fishing to me. Those trout were just like the Coastal Cutthroat Trout illustration in *Handbook No. 5*. "To the sportsman the cut-throat is of great value as a game fish," said the entry accompanying the picture. I knew that to be an understatement; sea-run cutthroat to me had become the most beautiful and desirable of all coastal fish. They were what made me a fly fisher.

I killed six of the trout that day, and Jon kept both of his; their blood ran dark over our hands. I could have kept several more fish, because bag limits were liberal and angling pressure was light. But I knew Haig-Brown preached environmental stewardship, and I had often seen the fly fishers I watched kneeling in the shallows to let their trout go. So I decided to follow their example and release some of my catch. The day I became a fly fisher, I learned how to let fish go.

The first cutthroat I released lay calm in my hands after the fight, and I looked at it in wonder. It was as if the painted trout in the guidebook, the work of art, had come to life. When I loosened my grip, it shot across the shallows.

It was a moment of disclosure for me. I had taken a trout, held it, cherished its beauty—and then just let it go. Instead of feeling loss as the fish fled, I experienced a sense of completeness, of joy almost, of belonging to nature. I hadn't anticipated that. When I looked at the six trout I killed that day, I saw their colors fading, their skin wrinkling. But the six fish I released had gone flashing and bright back into the water.

I realized something. A dead fish is there, but it's gone, fading to nothing; a released fish is gone, but it's still there, bright and alive. After that I began to let most my fish go, and the memories of the released fish have often been stronger than those of the fish I killed.

If I caught a lot, I sometimes would bring one trout or salmon home for dinner, killing it quickly but reluctantly. Often I would let them all go, much to my mother's dismay. She'd always thought it a miracle her son could deliver fish fresh from the water to her kitchen and looked forward to when I brought some of my catch home. But she loved nature too and understood my growing disinclination to kill.

"How many did you catch today?" she'd ask when I came in empty-handed.

"Six or seven."

"One would be nice. Not too many. Just for a meal would be nice."

"Next time," I'd promise, and she'd raise her eyebrows in an I've-heard-that-before way and go back to the kitchen.

––––

NOT MANY PEOPLE PRACTICED catch-and-release fishing in the 1960s, however, and as the human population grew and sport fishing pressure increased, sea-run cutthroat trout soon began to fade from coastal streams. At the same time stocks were being overfished, logging was destroying watersheds, creating bare mountainsides that bled rivers of muck into streams. There are still places today where I can catch sea-run cutthroat near a river mouth, on an incoming tide, but they are fewer. Those fish used to be everywhere, and encountering them was as predictable as the tide itself. Haig-Brown's warnings of environmental diminishment had been right—but the erosion of nature came much faster than he ever imagined. In a single generation we went from having streams that were full of salmon, steelhead, and trout, to a situation where many runs were endangered. The rivers Haig-Brown fished on Vancouver Island have increasingly been closed to steelhead fishing because stocks are so low, and province-wide, sea-run cutthroat are a remnant of what they once were.

I fished in times of great abundance, but with a sense of foreboding, with a feeling that the magical world I was exploring was threatened by forces alien to nature. I couldn't understand what drove the destruction. I knew it was money, but the money went to so few, and the loss was suffered by so many. Comprehending the complexities of nature seemed easy compared to figuring out why society would allow forests to be clearcut and rivers destroyed when the economic benefits were so fleeting. I was awakening that year to the great diminishment of nature that was occurring around me, and to the unraveling of my parents' marriage. I could feel the ground eroding under my feet, slipping away as gravel does under wading boots in a river. But I fished and tried not to get weighed down by it, by the sadness, the apprehension. I tried to pretend the current wasn't there.

A
SMALL RUN

THE FIRST STEELHEAD I saw were dead.

It was fall. In those days not many people were fly fishing the small streams I explored, and few of the fly fishers I saw on the water were young. I had no one to teach me about steelhead, fish that from my books and magazines I thought could only be found in the fabled rivers, like the Dean, the Kispiox, or Haig-Brown's home water, the Campbell. Outdoors writers described steelhead as the ultimate game fish; elusive, beautiful, strong fighters, and, when found, willing to rise through the water to strike a drifted fly. I dreamed of catching one.

British Columbia's great steelhead rivers were much written about, but they were mostly a long way from where I lived, on the southern tip of Vancouver Island. The extent of my range outside Victoria was limited by how far my father was willing to go on a Sunday drive. It was a chance for us to talk, but the conversations were never revealing. He was a political reporter then, and his stories of maneuverings in the legislature or at city hall weren't of great interest to me.

His main recreation was playing poker with other report-ers and with the politicians he covered. But cards held no interest for me either. And he wasn't much interested in my school life, or whether I had any dreams for the future.

"You can be anything you want to be," he said. I mumbled that I wasn't sure what I wanted to do beyond playing rugby and fly fishing.

"Can't make a living doing that," he said. "Next year I can help get you a summer job as a copyboy back at the *Edmonton Journal*. You can take the train out to Alberta, and I have friends there who will put you up. After that, get through high school and if you want to go to university, I will pay the first year's tuition. Then you are on your own."

So that was it. My future was planned. But as we drove to the river that day I was more interested in studying the flies in my fly box.

Sometimes he'd drop me at the Sooke River while he went for a pint in the pub near the bridge. That river can now be elbow-to-elbow with fly fishers when the salmon return in October, but then I was a solitary figure, and he'd come back to the river sometimes to find me wading deep, alone with the fish swirling all around me. I'd have to wring the water out of my jeans before getting in the car.

"Catch your death of cold," my mother scolded when I came home, my pants, runners, and socks still soaked from wading.

"No," said my dad. "I think he's part fish."

As my fly fishing skills grew, so did my catch—salmon in the fall when they came in fresh from the Pacific, and bass and trout at other times of the year. It wasn't long before my father noticed.

"Show me how to use your spinning rod," he said to me one day as we drove to a lake where I'd caught a big bass on our last outing. I was surprised by his interest, but there was a dock near the car park that was a perfect casting platform. In a few minutes he was lobbing a lure out into the lake and retrieving it.

"Slower as you wind the line in," I told him. "Let the lure work down into the water a bit." He nodded and I left him to it. When I came back a few hours later he had a big trout on the dock and a proud smile.

"This is easy," he said with delight. He bought a fishing license after that, and whenever we went out he'd take my old spinning rod and fish waters close to the car, never going farther than he had to. Although he'd played soccer in England as a boy, I never knew him to run, play sports, or do anything physically demanding as an adult. He was content to fish alone on one pool all afternoon as he waited for me, and I'd often return to find him standing on the same rock where I'd left him hours before. He caught fish sometimes, and when he did he'd mock me for working so hard while he just waited for the fish to come to him. But staying on one pool wasn't of interest to me. I had a desire for unknown water and was happiest ranging out as far as I could go, exploring every bend and pool in the stream, wading through the summer and late into October.

On one small stream in Sooke I found a perfect dogleg pool an easy walk from the highway bridge and took my father there. I could read the river and knew the current would carry his spinner along a deep run where salmon would hold before heading upstream.

"Cast to the head of the pool and let the current ride your lure through that slot," I said. I tied on a spinner for him, big enough to attract a coho but small enough that a sea-run cutthroat might take it.

I left him there to fish while I waded upstream and down, clambered over boulders, slipped under branches bending close to the water, and found cutthroat trout and coho salmon hiding in dark slots. I had made several trips to the stream before and I thought I knew all of its secrets. I felt a special closeness to it. It was becoming my new home water.

———

COMING BACK TO THE CAR late that afternoon I met another fisher who had parked near the bridge. It was rare to see anyone else fishing that stream, and I wondered if he'd stopped because he'd seen my dad's car in the pullout, so I stopped to talk to him.

The fisherman clearly knew what he was doing. He was dressed in bulky rubber waders, with a plaid lumberjack shirt tucked under suspenders. He had a heavy rod and a level wind reel, and he was casting a bobber and a hook baited with salmon eggs. It was a version of the simple bait-casting outfit I'd started with as a boy.

"How'd you do?" he asked. He had a ruddy, windblown face and a stubble of white whiskers. Friendly, plain, fishing alone like me.

"Some nice cutthroat, a few coho," I replied, feeling a kinship because we waded the same stream.

He looked for the fish.

"Let 'em all go," I said.

"Any steelhead?" he asked.

"No. There aren't any steelhead in this stream," I said.

"Oh yeah," he said. "A small run." He walked around his car and opened the trunk.

And there was the most painfully beautiful brace of fish I had ever seen, or ever would. The steelhead, glistening wet from the river, were lying one over the other, head to tail, as if passing in a pool drained of water. They had fat white bellies and slick green backs covered with black speckles. They were thick as fire logs, nearly twice the size of the five-pound coho I'd been catching. They were perfect fish, wondrous in their symmetry; a matched pair on their way to spawn.

I was stunned. I should have known about the steelhead run in that stream. And I should have been the one to catch them, but somehow I had waded blindly past them, unaware they were hiding in the darkness, like secrets do. I felt ashamed that I didn't know this detail about my home stream, but also sadness that such rare, beautiful fish had been killed. There they were—the mythical steelhead I had read about, meat-counter dead. I thought, but out of politeness didn't say: "Why didn't you let them go?"

I usually felt a sense of lightness when I went fly fishing, a physical lifting-up, as if there were less gravity on the water. But that day I felt melancholy, and over my life it has been a feeling that has often returned on steelhead rivers, where so many stocks have become endangered or are extirpated. I can trace that feeling of loss, that pensive sadness, further back, to my childhood in the scrubland forests of Alberta, where I first sensed how easily things could be damaged in the natural world. In life, as in families.

———

STEELHEAD RUNS WOULD SOON VANISH from my home stream and many other small creeks on Vancouver Island.

Those waters historically may have had as few as thirty steelhead spawning in them. Nobody knows for sure, but it didn't take much to wipe them out. Too many steelhead were killed by anglers and put in car trunks, too many by commercial salmon nets, and the rest were lost when logging led to watershed erosion. So much soil ran off the clearcut mountains that spawning beds were paved with silt, smothering fish eggs incubating in the gravel.

It wasn't just the small, fragile streams that suffered. On many of the big steelhead rivers in British Columbia, including the ones made famous by Haig-Brown's writings, the numbers declined so drastically that the government mandated that all wild steelhead had to be released. And when that didn't work, some rivers were closed to steelhead fishing. On the Thompson River, steelhead stocks fell over my lifetime from a historic high of twenty thousand fish to less than two hundred. From startling abundance to a biological vanishing point in less than one human generation.

Haig-Brown didn't see that coming; not that quickly, not in that magnitude. Neither did I, though I did have a sense of foreboding the day the old man closed the trunk and the steelhead were gone forever.

I walked away from the angler and went to find my father, who was where I'd left him. He'd been happily casting for hours on the dogleg pool, and now had a beautiful coho lying on the rocks beside him. It was a big fish and he was proud of it. He was becoming a fisherman.

———

THAT WAS ONE OF THE last times we went fishing there together. Soon after that trip my mother told me she and my father were separating.

"He has moved out," she said bitterly when I came home from classes at university and found her crying, alone in the kitchen.

My father didn't have much to say about it later. "People change," he said, after putting his suitcase in the car. "We just grew apart. This is best for all." Then he drove off.

I could see his point, but wondered where the blame for the alienation in their relationship lay. While he had pursued a dynamic career in journalism that saw him go on assignments to Europe and Asia, that brought him in contact with prime ministers, premiers, and top business executives, she had stayed at home, cloistered, focusing all of herself on raising their children. Her work left him completely free to pursue his career—and left her in isolation. An intellectual and emotional gulf opened between them.

Always certain of his judgment, he had a finality in his voice when he said he was moving on. It was clear he wasn't looking back, and I felt it pointless to argue. Soon he was living with a much younger woman who had a professional career and a world experience that matched his. My mother, who had lived through the World War II bombing of England without damage, seemed shell-shocked by the development, but mostly she was silent about what had happened between them.

After my father left her, she stayed for a while in the family home, confused and exhausted, wandering like a ghost in a big, rambling house that had slowly been emptying out. In the preceding years three of my brothers—Steve, a poet and journalist, Tim, an artist and rancher, and Andy, a photographer and media consultant—had found jobs in other cities and left home. I was a university student, walking to the campus near where we lived and paying my second-year tuition by editing the student newspaper. Jon, the youngest, was working on the water as a cash buyer of herring, which took him away for long periods, following the fleet into the Gulf of Alaska.

I didn't know how to help my mother. But she was a quiet woman with a hidden toughness, and one day she announced she had found a job, a live-in housekeeping position at a small hotel just outside Victoria, and she was moving out too.

"I don't intend to play the abandoned woman," she said, her two small suitcases packed and sitting in the hall.

Just like that, she was gone, and Jon came home from the sea to find he and I were left in a house of empty rooms, vanishing memories, and untold stories.

"Well, that's a helluva deal," said Jon as we sat together at the old oak table that had come around the Horn to Penticton and at which our family had crowded for so many busy meals, in so many homes. Jon was still a teenager, but he had grown into a big man with his tough job on the fishing boats. He looked solid, but I could feel him crumple inside as we listened to the emptiness of the house and thought about what the separation of our parents meant.

"I just jammed all of my emotions inside and let them fester," he would say later.

For both of us the sudden change was disorienting and bewildering. Our home was rented and with both parents gone, soon the bills fell to us. I dropped out of university at the end of that year so that I could get a job, and I moved into a house with friends. Jon stayed at home for a while, sharing rent with a rugby team that needed a clubhouse. Then he moved on too.

LIFE DOES NOT PASS IN steady, sequential segments. It speeds up and slows down like a river, has deep pockets and shallows, and some of it is just a blur. You can drown if you are not careful. For me the decade that followed spun out so quickly it was like line being pulled off a reel by a heavy weight. Through my twenties I rushed through a series of newspaper jobs and too many relationships, including a short, broken marriage of my own that ended in chaos, but without children. I had just begun to think about starting a family when the relationship unraveled with such speed it left me questioning if anything was dependable, including myself. As I packed my own suitcase and moved into a hotel, any thoughts I had of being a father evaporated. After that I drifted away from the water, concentrated on work, and lost touch with something fundamental to who I was.

One day, packing for yet another move to another job, I found my fly rod, stored in an aluminum tube at the back of a closet. The silver metal was the color of a salmon and it was cold to the touch. I dug out my fly boxes, my waders, and thought of the rivers and lakes I had fished. I knew that I would have to find my way back to them.

II
OVERFLOW

"Everything flows and nothing stays...
You can't step twice into the same river."

HERACLITUS, Greek philosopher,
c. 540–c. 480 BCE

SAINT JOSEPH

THE ORANGE LAND CRUISER with a green canvas canoe on its roof rack rattled and pinged as gravel spit against its undercarriage. Behind us a cloud of summer dust trailed, lingering fine and smoky in the air, flagging our route on a logging road through the remnants of a forest toward the San Josef River, on the north end of Vancouver Island.

Maggie and I slowed at a bridge, big wooden beams clunking under the truck's weight, and looked down into glassy green water. Gray stones speckled like the backs of salmon and solid black stones where all the light vanished formed the riverbed. Made smooth by centuries of running water, they had been placed by spring floods and each was exactly where it had to be.

Cedar boughs dipped from the riverbank, reflecting green on the water, and under the shade of the stately trees fern fronds nodded like a flock of feeding birds. Out the passenger side window Maggie saw a merganser splashing upstream with nine chicks, freshly hatched but already adept at skittering across the water.

For a few minutes we drove through a grove of ancient trees, marveling at their size, but it was just a small patch left from a once-great forest that had been broken down and shipped away. Logging is the technical term, but "smash and grab" might be a better way to describe how forests are cut. We drove on through miles of slash, where shattered tree trunks and branches lay in great piles. The contrast between the logged and unlogged areas was dramatic.

"My god," said Maggie, who was visiting me from Ontario and who hadn't seen a clearcut in British Columbia before. "Utter devastation. Aren't there laws against this?"

There weren't. Maggie had grown up in Pine Falls, Manitoba, where her father ran a pulp mill, so she knew that active logging zones aren't pretty. But the scale of clearcutting in British Columbia, where entire mountainsides were stripped, was shocking.

"Where do the birds go?" she asked. "Where do the animals go?"

Surrounding us was a vast area of smoothly sawed stumps with centuries of growth rings exposed, piles of torn branches and shattered tree trunks stacked higher than houses: the typical rubble of industrial logging. Later we drove back into big timber again when we entered the protected land of Cape Scott Provincial Park. It was cooler in the shade of the forest and we heard the whispering trills of a flock of pine siskins passing overhead.

That was a summer of discovery for us. We'd met a year earlier while I was working in Ottawa as a political journalist and Maggie was a national science correspondent. We were both in a newsroom on Parliament Hill. On weekends we went into the countryside and walked through the woods together. She identified birds for me, and I pointed out a porcupine feeding high in an aspen. Standing on a dock one fall afternoon, the trees blazing bright around us, I saw the shadow of a fish.

"Watch this," I said.

I pulled a nickel out of my pocket and flipped it into the water. As it tumbled down, flashing in the weak sunlight, a smallmouth bass darted out and nipped at the coin. We laughed. I told her stories of salmon rivers, of bears and great forests. And later I told her that I was quitting my job in Ottawa and returning to the West Coast. She said she would come out to British Columbia sometime. To see me again after I left. I didn't know what I was looking for in going back. But I knew it would be found on the water.

Several months passed and then Maggie came for a visit, searching for me, wondering if I had found the peace I sought. She wanted to find out if she loved me enough to leave her job and move to the coast, and I didn't know what to say about that, about risking a career for something as unpredictable as a relationship. I thought maybe the best thing for us to do was to just travel through the wilds together. To see where it led.

———

THE ROAD ENDED AT A smooth, dark river. We slid the canoe off the roof, loaded it with camping gear, and launched.

"It's tidal here. We can't be far from the ocean," I said as we paddled past low-hanging tree branches draped with strands of seaweed, as soft and damp as a mermaid's hair.

Maggie inhaled; held her breath. "I can smell the sea," she said, happy to be away from the city. There was big timber on both banks: Douglas fir, spruce, one old, solemn cedar. In the distance we could see something moving upstream toward us. Maggie dug out her birding binoculars.

"It's two men in a boat."

It looked like an ungainly sea creature, struggling to come ashore. As we drifted closer I saw the men were in an inflatable canoe that was bending in the middle under their weight. They had kayak paddles and were slapping the water wildly.

"Good timing for you," shouted the man in the bow. "You've got the tide."

They were coming up against an increasingly strong current and we were going down with it.

"How far to the sea?" I asked.

"About half an hour for us. You'll be there in ten minutes," said one of the men, not pausing his furious paddle strokes.

We drifted through a section where waist-high marsh grass stood on either bank and watched a pair of river otters swim toward us. When they saw the canoe, one went to shore and disappeared into a dark crevice. The other dove and swam underneath us, its route marked by a string of silver bubbles.

Ahead we heard the steady thud and hiss of surf and the cries of gulls spinning in the air. Maggie looked with her binoculars. "Glaucous-winged; mew. Not sure. Lots of them, twirling round," she said.

There was a long sweep of sand to the north, and to the south a rocky shore. The bay was gently curved, with rock pillars known as sea stacks in the distance on one shoreline, and forested mountains rising up into a blue sky on the other. Far out, the bay widened into the Pacific, vast under a lumpy mass of clouds along a curved horizon.

On the beach there was a bright-orange tarp stretched over a gap in a pile of drift logs, creating a lean-to. Six people were sitting around the entrance. An older man and one in his early twenties came out of the trees nearby. They had their arms around each other; the older one seemed unsteady and the younger one, overly loud from drinking, was propping him up. The people at the camp shouted to them. Someone laughed. Nearby two teenaged girls sat on the beach, stretching their legs so the water touched their feet just where the waves slid back.

In front of us surf broke heavy on a sandbar.

"We can't canoe out through those big waves," I said. "But we can line down the shore until we find a quiet camping spot."

"Let's go a long way," said Maggie, glancing at the tarp camp. She got out to wade, waves slopping up to soak her shorts, and pulled the canoe through the shallows, the boat rolling up over each wave. When the tarp camp was far behind us we set up our tent near a jumble of drift logs tossed high on the beach by winter storms. A sea stack, moss covered and with small trees growing on its crown, stood nearby. The beach stretched before us, lined with a ribbon of foaming surf. The waves fell all at once with a percussive thud.

That evening the wind blew hard and steady, and we saw the salmon fleet come scudding in just at dark, their lights twinkling in the rigging. The boats lay in shelter along the far shore, using the forest and mountain as a windbreak.

"I can't believe how beautiful it all is," Maggie said. In the city we always had intense discussions about work, but now that all seemed so distant, so unimportant. Life here was as simple as breathing.

"I've missed this," she said, and I realized what I had missed was sharing nature with someone who helped anchor me. I felt like she was pulling me back to earth. The surf boomed all night and we slept late the next morning. The warmth of the sun woke us, the tent rustling gently in the wind like a woman's dress.

People from the orange tarp wandered by on occasion: an old man and young girl berry picking; two young men, one chasing the other and swearing, the people at the lean-to, loud with alcohol, shouting after them. We decided they were best avoided.

The sun shone day after day. Far out at sea we could see a bank of fog, slumbering and soft, but inside the bay the air was clear and the water hard blue. During the night a bear had left a perfect set of tracks along the beach. I called Maggie over to look at the paw prints, then we heard the bear in the woods. A single twig snapped, and I could imagine the bear's weak eyes in the cool shadows trying to make us out on the dazzling white sand. I threw a rock and heard the bear run off, clumsy as it crashed through the brush. Maggie laughed in surprise. "Not very graceful," she said, as the bear blundered through the forest.

Forty minutes later the bear (or another one) was back, walking along the beach toward us. It was moving quickly, head down, swinging side to side.

"Uh-oh," I said to Maggie, and this time we gave way, moving to a rocky outcrop near the water. The bear ambled toward our camp until I whistled, sharp and insistent, then it paused, turned, and ran down the beach toward the orange tarp before plunging into the sheltering forest.

That afternoon, when the shadow of the sea stack fell across the tent, cooling the fabric, we went in and lay in the shade. There was only the sound of surf and Maggie breathing gently against my cheek. It was hard to tell where the power of the ocean ended.

The evening was peaceful, the surf subsiding, no wind for a moment, the sun glowing twenty-four shades of orange as it set behind the Pacific. I sat against a drift log, scanning the bay as I waited for the campfire to burn down to cooking coals. You see wondrous things when you search with binoculars; the unexpected materializes out of nothing. I saw a deer come out of the woods, move gingerly across the beach, and swim to the far shore. I saw a bear turning over rocks, searching for crabs. There were seal heads appearing and disappearing, diving birds coming up slick with water, and in the distance spray plumes of whales. As I glassed the bay a salmon jumped high above the shining sea, its belly white, its back blue. Just a flash, then it was gone.

A few commercial fishing boats were back, anchoring along the far shore where they had been the night before. It was too far to make out what they were doing, but I could see figures near the stern and thought they must be cleaning their catch, the guts going over the side in plumes of blood. Gulls wheeled above the boat. The crabs would gather below to feed. I looked out to the horizon, where a gentle blue light glowed in the sky. Night was coming.

———

THE NEXT MORNING WE TOOK a mountain trail that led us high on a ridge where we hoped to look down on a protected bay said to hold sea otters. But a rain cloud drifted in from the Pacific, hiding the sea. Tendrils of mist caught in the branches, condensed into dew, and dripped to the ground. The forest grew cool around us, and we couldn't see the bay where we'd hoped to spot the sea otters. Getting cold and wet in the clouds, we retreated through the forest, going back down the mountain trail to the beach and summer again.

That afternoon we broke camp, timing our departure so a rising tide would push us back up the river. We drove out the way we'd come in, through the clearcuts to Port Hardy, and caught one ferry to Prince Rupert, then another to Haida Gwaii, an archipelago off British Columbia's northern coast.

We crossed on an old ferry, scanning the water for shark fins and trying to identify flocks of seabirds hurtling past on the wind. At Queen Charlotte City we walked along Wharf Way, Maggie talking to everyone and smiling about the friendliness of small towns, with strangers telling us where to look for whales and where to find the best beaches.

A fly fisher's eyes are always watching the water, and shortly after we drove out of Queen Charlotte City I pulled the truck to a stop on the roadside.

"There's something there," I said, pointing to the bay. On one patch of sea it looked like there was a gentle upwelling, as if there were an underwater spring coming to the surface. Gulls were swirling over the ripples, and Maggie looked through her binoculars to see if the birds were attacking a school of baitfish.

Slowly a whale came up, its gray back breaking the blue ocean. It blew a plume of shimmering spray that hung for a moment like a veil of tiny fish scales. Then the whale humped its back and went down: an island sinking. It was feeding on something below, schools of krill or spawning herring.

When the whale surfaced again it was so close we could hear it exhale—*poosh*—as the gulls cried in excitement and dove into the water, catching whatever was spilling from the whale's mouth. We watched for half an hour, then left it to its meal and drove on. There is always something more ahead to see on Haida Gwaii.

At the Tlell River we stopped so I could fish for sea-run cutthroat. It had been a long time since I'd done that. It felt good to cast a line across the water, to feel the meditative movement. I sank into the rhythm.

Just then a trout came up fast out of deep water to take my fly, striking so wildly it sprayed droplets across the surface. I brought it in splashing and vigorous. A small trout but perfectly formed, cold as the Pacific and heavily spotted. Under its jaws were two red slashes that marked it as a cutthroat.

I was thirty-four and hadn't taken a sea-run trout since I'd moved from the coast a decade before. It seemed like I'd looked away from the page for a moment and a whole chapter of my life had slipped past. I held the fish and remembered fishing on Muir Creek, when I was learning to fly cast, with my brother Jon wading into the water to net trout for me, and my dad on the riverbank watching. I felt a tug of sadness. Then I let it go; the memory and the fish both.

Maggie wandered through the sand dunes, near the river mouth, watching birds and standing with her arms spread while the wind tossed her hair and made her jacket flap. She was always smiling; eyes blue like the sea.

I was wading in the river, so close to the ocean I could hear the surf and feel the thud passing through the air.

WE CAMPED AT NORTH BEACH, where a Haida creation legend says the first humans emerged from a giant clamshell. When you are there, looking through the mist to the islands of the Alaska Panhandle, it is easy enough to believe.

We gathered Pacific razor clams, digging after them in the soppy sand, plunging our hands into the murk until we felt the rough texture of a shell, and then we pulled them up into the light. And we caught Dungeness crabs in a shallow bay, wading waist-deep in the ocean. On a rocky outcrop Maggie reached into a tide pool, dipping her hands through her own reflection and the reflection of the blue sky above.

"Look," she said, holding in her cupped hands silver water and a tiny octopus with mottled skin. The light shone through its translucent body. It was like a piece of red glass that moved. She lowered her hands back into the pool and the octopus, gangly legged, reaching for anything it could find in eight directions at once, drifted to the bottom and disappeared under a rock. It pulled itself into nothing, like a shadow escaping light.

Maggie looked up, amazed, delighted. Catch-and-release octopus fishing.

After leaving Haida Gwaii we drove inland, to follow the Skeena River through the Coast Range. We stopped in Moricetown, on the Bulkley River, to watch Wet'suwet'en fishers catching salmon in the white water pouring through Witset Canyon. Black rocks pressed the river and the salmon together in tight seams of current. The Wet'suwet'en found the fish with long dip nets, feeling in the turbid water for the bump of a passing school. They lifted the netted salmon up with shouts of joy.

We went to a smokehouse where a Wet'suwet'en elder sold us strips of dried fish she had rolled up like Dead Sea Scrolls. I thought, if you could read them, they would tell a story of endless journeys; they would tell the story of creation.

"Just heat it up over the campfire and the oil will come out and it will unfold and be delicious," she said. "You aren't undercover fisheries agents, are you?" she asked, searching my face for assurance before taking our money. Nearby a man in a plaid shirt, scuffed cowboy boots, and jeans held up by a heavy silver buckle leaned back on a wooden chair, a guitar in his lap.

"This is for you," he said to Maggie, singing a ballad about a cowboy and a lonesome road. The couple waved as we drove off, the smell of smoked salmon in the truck.

———

MANY OF BRITISH COLUMBIA'S BACK ROADS had been closed that summer due to massive wildfires. Because of global warming there had been a series of mild winters and pine beetle swarms had erupted, leaving behind dying, tinder-dry forests. Fires had flared across British Columbia's vast landscape, but then it rained hard for three days and the fire risk fell, although blue smoke still hung in the air. Just as we approached the turnoff to Bowron Lake Provincial Park, we heard on the radio that the backcountry travel ban had been lifted. The park has one of the world's best canoe circuits along a chain of lakes in the Cariboo mountain range, and there is often a long waiting list on the reservation registry. But the fires had disrupted everyone's plans that summer. We turned off the highway, drove to the park office, and asked if we could get a permit to paddle the route.

"There are only two parties out there," said the ranger. "You'll pretty much have it to yourselves."

So we launched our canoe on ruffled waters with gray clouds streaming overhead. We didn't have time to paddle the full circuit but could go out for a few days. That evening a heavy rainstorm caught us on Swan Lake as we were looking for a designated campsite. It was hard to make out any features on the shoreline through the rain. Then we spotted a moose in the distance, standing on the water's edge, its tawny color distinct against a foggy green backdrop. It gave me a target to steer by, and we headed for it across the lake. When we pulled in, the animal was gone, but it had been on the beach right next to the campsite we were looking for.

"An omen," I said. "It guided us here."

We could see a clearing in the trees where the tent pad was and scrambled ashore. The rain paused for a few minutes, and we got the tent up and went in laughing just as the next onslaught fell. Rain rattled on the tent roof, the wind driving it down hard at times. Rivulets ran along creases in the fabric, pooled, and then spilled out with a splash. We zipped our sleeping bags together and lay close, letting the weather run its course.

"I love storms," I said as the tent shuddered, but Maggie didn't answer. She was already asleep.

The next day we saw eagles perched along the Bowron River. Every hundred yards there was an eagle in a tree, shoulders hunched, looking down into the water.

"They are watching for salmon," I said.

So we paddled up the slow river, looking for the red backs of sockeye. The run wasn't in yet, but the eagles spiraled out sometimes over the lake and then came back to the river, which made me think they could see salmon coming. They knew the fish could be caught when they reached the shallow river.

After stopping on a gravel bar for lunch, we turned back, drifting downstream silently. Then, at a tight corner, a bear came out of the bushes on the bank. Brown and amber with a dished face, it was about fifty feet ahead of us, so close I didn't want to speak. I leaned forward to touch Maggie with my paddle. She looked back, saw me put my fingers to my lips and point. We drifted toward the bear until it was directly above us. Then it stood on its hind legs, rising out of the willows with its forepaws dangling. It was only about fifteen feet away, so close that with one jump it could have been in the canoe.

The bear snuffed loudly, tipped her nose up, searching for our scent, fur bristling on her neck, muscles tensing, mouth partly open. Then she spun, dropped to all fours, and bolted into the bush, the tops of the willows shaking, branches breaking as she ran straight through the thicket.

Maggie looked back at me, her eyes wide. She had been holding her breath and let it out now in a rush. I had the canoe paddle up, where I had stopped mid-stroke. We didn't speak until we'd drifted around the bend, then both talked at once, trying to slow our hearts.

"That bear was so close," said Maggie. "I was looking up at its belly. And its claws were so huge."

"That was a grizzly," I said. "Closest I've ever been to one."

"A grizzly?" she said. "And you never got that close before?"

"Never."

"Never want to again," she said, though I knew she didn't regret it happening.

Paddling down the lake to camp we saw the moose again far away, on the shoreline by our tent. But when we got closer, Maggie put up her binoculars.

"That's no moose," she said. It was another grizzly bear, twice the size of the one on the river, pacing on the beach. It left slowly as we came in, walking reluctantly into the forest and looking back as if it might change its mind, then it was hidden by bushes.

The sand was scuffed where it had paced back and forth. Salmon would come into that bay when the run arrived, perhaps to spawn in the lakeshore shallows if there were underwater springs in the gravel, and a bear might catch a fish there. Like the eagles, the grizzly bears were waiting for the sockeye.

We nervously went ashore and took down the tent, looking into the woods for movement. Then I walked into the forest to retrieve our food, cached up a tree. I thought I could smell the bear, its heat shadow musky as fresh-turned soil.

Earlier that day we had paddled past an old log cabin near the mouth of Bowron River and I said we could move there.

"It was probably built by a trapper or prospector fifty years ago," I said. "But it should be solid."

"It has a door," said Maggie. So we moved in for a few nights. Mice feet pattered on the roof like soft rain, and each evening a bull moose came out of the forest to feed on aquatic plants in the lake. When it lifted its head, water streamed from its antlers. During the day I fished for small trout in beaver ponds nearby, watching for bears.

Leaving the park we paddled against the wind to the takeout and, before loading the canoe, took a self-timed photo, resting the camera on the truck hood. In the picture we both look tanned, happy from seeing grizzly bears, and strong from paddling.

We drove south from Bowron Lake, taking our time getting back to Vancouver. The route wound through forests and along rivers, and we took back roads, camped on lakes. Sometimes we'd drift in the canoe, a small fly trailing behind us, and I would catch a rainbow trout for dinner. The fish spit and crackled in the frying pan, and the white flesh had a delicate, sweet taste.

When we finally reached the city, it felt, for the first time, like we were coming home together, and I tried not to think about the outbound flight to Ottawa that Maggie was booked on.

At the airport we held each other gently. Maggie said I smelled like campfire smoke. Then she was gone. I had lived an itinerant life for as long as I could remember, routinely leaving towns, homes, jobs, and friends behind with little remorse. But this felt different. I stood at the airport for a long time after the plane left, wondering what I could do to change this trajectory, to stop this wandering. I had told Maggie before she left that I felt like I belonged on the West Coast, that the mountains and the salmon rivers were part of me. But I wondered if I would be uprooted again, if I would leave to follow her.

In Ottawa, Maggie thought about the forests and the ocean, the tiny, undulating glass octopus, and the wild bears as big as tents, and she called to say she had decided to come back, to live with me in British Columbia. Or at least to try it out. To see what would happen. And what happened soon after would change us both. A genesis of someone new had traveled with us, up the coast, through the mountains, and on the Bowron River, where she passed with us under the shadow of a grizzly bear.

Maggie always said the conception could not be pinpointed precisely, but I insisted on tracing it back, down that dusty logging road, to the bay named after Saint Joseph. It did seem a miracle.

TWO

SOMEWHERE DOWN THE HALL a woman screamed, a deep, piercing cry, releasing pain. I felt my throat constrict. Then there was another sound from the room next to ours. Guttural. It sounded like a bear coughing in the woods. I was in the birthing unit at BC Women's Hospital and was about to become a father.

In our room Maggie undressed quietly. She was serene, and the cries of labor down the hall that shook me didn't seem to trouble her. I was in a woman's domain and to her these were sounds not of fear, but of strength, affirmation, and union. As she slid onto the bed, her stomach tight as a drum, I tried to remember the birthing lessons we'd had at St. Paul's Hospital, where one day a technician had shown me an ultrasound picture. Only then, confronted by a murky black-and-white image, the outline of life under water, did the magnitude of what was happening come into focus for me. Until that moment the baby had seemed across an unfathomable divide, within her mother but somehow unreal, as distant as a wandering comet. I held the small picture in my hands, then reached out to touch Maggie. The fetus was there, floating in amniotic fluid, so close I could feel it move, radiating heat through her skin.

At the foot of the birthing bed was a bar covered with compressed sponge for a woman in labor to grab hold of. I tried to imagine the position: the mother gripping the bar, feet braced, pulling her body forward and pushing back from the baby at the same time. It seemed rational, sort of, but incomprehensible too. I was trying to think things through, but was about to learn that despite all the lessons, the books, the diagrams, the Hollywood depictions of childbirth that I'd been exposed to, I had no idea what was really going to happen. Looking down I saw where fingernails had ripped the soft covering on the birthing bar. And next to where my uncertain hand rested was a jagged, deep impression left by a full set of teeth: incisors, canines, molars. A woman had tried to bite through the bar, the way a wolf might.

I listened to the screams down the hall and thought: a storm is about to hit.

I will not write much more about how a man experiences birth, because that is the place of women, except to say that I felt rising trepidation, anxiety, uncertainty—and fear.

Then it began.

The midwife and Maggie worked together through the first stage of labor while the doctor came and went, offering advice as hours followed hours. Maggie grew exhausted during transition to the second stage and still the baby wouldn't come, stopping in the birth canal, just short of emergence. But when the doctor brought out obstetrical forceps, intending to grasp our baby by the head and pull her into the world, the midwife told him to put the instrument away.

"This baby is coming naturally," she said with a finality that could not be challenged. It was as if she had driven a knife into the table between them. The doctor nodded, stepped back; we waited.

"Okay," said Maggie, and gripping the bed rail, she tried again to move the weight inside her.

And then Emma emerged, slid from her mother, was lifted, wiped, and moments later lay on Maggie's chest and began to suckle.

An estimated 353,000 babies are born every day on Earth, a little more than four every second. With nearly eight billion people in the world, having babies is obviously something women are very good at. Birthing is such a natural process that most animal species just casually integrate it into their lives. Caribou give birth while they are walking and bears while they are sleeping. But it is a more complex process for humans, and the medical methods we use, at least in the First World, have become increasingly elaborate. Most women go into hospitals where they are watched over by doctors and nurses, monitored by machines, their babies scanned repeatedly by ultrasound technology, every stage of development tracked and recorded. Parents are given pictures of life evolving in the womb. The sex can be told long before birth, and scans are made for chromosomal disorders, heart defects, or a dozen other problems.

It used to be far less involved. Through most of history women gave birth without any medical help, but it is no less a miracle when it takes place in a hospital with all the assistance of modern medicine. Witnessing it is transformative, revelatory, numinous; as bewildering as being thrown from a rooftop and landing on your feet. At that moment the earth may feel solid beneath you, unmoving, but everything has somehow changed in that dizzy fall from the sky.

In the birthing room that morning a lifetime of media images that had shaped my perception of women as gentle objects of allure were displaced by the singular reality of one woman, screaming life into being. That ferocity, once witnessed, is not an image any man can let go of, or wants to. The baby gasps. The first breath is a miracle; then the cry for life. A new voice, never heard before, awakening me as much as herself. Dazed, bewildered, exhausted, I lay on a gurney next to Maggie, who had already fallen into a deep sleep.

"Hey, it is okay to go home now. She'll be fine," the midwife said later when I stirred. "They'll both be fine."

We had gone to the hospital in the afternoon, and now the sun was coming up at 5:30 AM. I saw the light spreading across the city as I drove through empty streets, my heart pounding. I thought it had rained, on just one side of the road. Then a city truck went past, washing the pavement, and I realized my brain wasn't processing information very well. I couldn't piece the simplest facts together. I drove slowly after that, afraid of crashing.

At home I sat in our small apartment near False Creek, where our baby would soon rest in an empty sock drawer on the floor next to the bed. I stared out the window, waiting for a decent hour before calling family and friends. Impatient for them to awaken because, really, who could be sleeping on such an important day? I started calling at 6:30 AM and woke a few people that morning.

"Hey, Maggie had a baby girl last night. She's good and the baby is beautiful," I said.

The men congratulated me, as if I had actually done something. The women asked questions I couldn't answer, about the length of labor, about what the midwife said, about how the baby presented, and her exact weight at birth. I stumbled through the answers because all that was a blur to me. The gender and name I knew: "Emma," I said.

A day later Maggie and I walked out of the hospital. She let me carry Emma, tiny and wrapped tight in swaddling. As the automatic doors slid open I hesitated. Surely an official was going to stop me and ask if I knew what I was doing. Had I taken a fatherhood course? Did I know how to hold a baby? To feed a baby? To change a baby? Did I even know what to do when a baby cried?

I didn't, except what I'd read in books. But no one stopped us. Maggie smiled at me, gestured to the door, and we went out: the three of us.

We strapped Emma into a car seat in the back and Maggie sat beside her all the way home. It felt different when we got inside the house. It felt like nothing existed outside anymore, like all the planets of the universe now orbited around this one, small point of light cradled in our arms.

A few days later I went to the human resources office at work and asked for my personnel form so I could add a dependent. For the first time I wrote about myself the word "father" and about Emma the word "daughter." I had never before felt joy filling out a form. But now it was official. I was a dad. I smiled as I checked the box.

A week later our landlord saw Maggie on the front steps, holding Emma.

"What's that?" he asked.

"It's our baby."

"It's an adults only apartment," he said. "You'll have to move."

That night over dinner we talked about whether or not to fight the eviction in court.

"We could win," I said. "But do we have the energy for that? Do we want that kind of vexation in our lives right now?"

"No," said Maggie, cradling Emma. "It's time we had our own home."

So we started looking and within a few weeks found a two-bedroom, eighty-year-old house set under some big trees, across from a small park with a basketball court, where teenage boys played late into the night with laughter and the ball ringing off the rim. An elementary school was just a few blocks away.

FROM THE MOMENT OUR FIRST CHILD was born Maggie held her as naturally as a bough holds a bird's nest. But it took time for me to learn how to carry a baby with confidence, to escape the feeling that I would squeeze her too tightly or hold her too loosely and drop her.

I took a deep breath, lifted Emma to my chest, and was afraid to move. She weighed almost nothing; her pale, puffy face was serene, her eyes closed, with tiny, almost invisible lashes turned up toward me. After a few minutes I handed her back, still amazed that Maggie had created another life and that she had such trust in knowing how to nurture something so delicate.

Gradually I grew at ease holding Emma. I cradled her against my chest as I walked with her or rested her in my lap while watching hockey games on TV. Soon she seemed just a part of me, lying with her head on my chest, listening to my heart, as I read the daily newspaper or as I walked slowly with her through Trout Lake Park, a few blocks from our new home in East Vancouver. She slept blissfully, as we do when held with love.

Her first bed was in a dresser drawer lined with a sheep-skin rug. We set it on the floor next to the bed and during the night I would wake, lean over, and listen to her breathing, seeking reassurance that she was still there. When she awoke Maggie would lift her up to suckle and lie wrapped in the warmth of her body.

EMMA WAS BORN IN THE SPRING and she went on her first camping trip that summer, her blue eyes staring wide at the sky. Her first campout was on Island Lake as we drove the back roads to a family reunion. It was a few years before a major highway, the Okanagan Connector, would be built over the mountains from Merritt to Peachland, so we followed old logging roads through the pine forests, the air rich with the smell of needles, bark, and conifer resin. Every time we hit a bump Maggie would turn back to make sure Emma was secure in her baby seat.

On one long, muddy grade I looked in the rearview mirror and saw the rutted tracks the truck was leaving, saw the vast expanse of woodlands stretching out behind us, shadows between endless green trees, and realized how far I had taken my family into the wilderness, that if we got stuck now it wasn't just a matter of Maggie and me hiking out. Emma was there, burbling in the car seat. In that moment the weight of having someone who was fully and completely dependent on my decisions fell on me.

The realization I was becoming a father had hit when I saw the first fetal ultrasound. That sketchy sonogram, showing a baby curled up in Maggie's womb, conveyed to me what until then had only been an abstraction: that a separate life would soon be joined to ours. But becoming a father and learning fatherhood are different things, just as learning to fly cast is not the same as learning how to fish. One is merely physical—you lift the rod and throw the line—but the other is intuitive and metaphysical. It awakens in you; an understanding that there is something larger going on and that you can become part of it. Then the light comes in. It was on that lonely, muddy logging road that I first saw that my life was not a single thread anymore, that everything I did now had repercussions for my daughter. Maggie and I had become braided strands, interlaced with Emma, and we could not be unwound.

Just then the truck slithered in the mud, and I saw how narrow the shoulder was, how hazardous the slope, how boundless the forest that lay around us. In the past I would have ignored the risk, stepped on the gas and raced uphill with soft, wet earth spraying behind the truck. But I knew if we slid off the road and mired, we could not hike to the nearest highway before dark. I could sleep under a windfall easily enough, rise stiffly at dawn, and walk out; but such a boy's misadventure would be punishingly hard for a baby and new mother.

Queasy about where the truck might slide, I geared down, eased off the gas, and searched for solid ground. I tried to sense where the four wheels were as they sloughed mud, the treads clawing at the pulpy road. I was finding my way.

The truck slowed. I kept nudging the gas pedal, keeping just enough speed to push through the slop, but not so much that we slid. Holding momentum. We crawled up the mountain road, crested the hill, and got on drier ground. I started to breathe steadily again. Behind I could see the snaking tire tracks I'd left on the muddy slope against a background of vast forest.

After that we found the road to Paradise Lake, then a spur that led to Island Lake. We set our blue tent on a deserted shoreline and paddled across the still waters in the canoe that Emma would spend so much of her early years in. We set her in a tiny yellow life jacket on a soft blanket on the red cedar planking between the thwarts, looking up at a new and beautiful world.

Trout swirled on the shining surface of the lake, rising to a caddis fly hatch that any other time would have captivated me. But I didn't fish that day. I couldn't take my attention away from paddling the canoe, which had become a cradle. So we drifted through the lily pads close to shore, listening to the dragonflies buzz around us. A startled deer caught our scent and vaulted through the underbrush, crashing off into the distance, the sound of its flight fading with each leap.

That night we lay in the tent with Emma between us, the rain fly off on a cloudless night so we could gaze through the sheer roof at the faint glimmer of the seasonal constellations. There were intermittent streaks of silver. Tiny pieces of the universe were burning in the Earth's atmosphere. We heard coyotes yelping in the distance, their calls rising from the forest and falling back into darkness. It seems in retrospect to have been a risky thing to do, to take such a small baby into the wild. But we didn't think that then; we just added Emma to the life we were living. We took her with us on the seasonal rounds.

FOUR YEARS AFTER I ENTERED BC Women's Hospital for Emma's birth, I crossed the same parking lot again, with Maggie moving slowly beside me.

"Let's walk around for a bit," she said. Then she stopped. "No. It's time. Let's go in now."

We went in, me feeling foolishly helpless again and nervous in the way one is when something charged with risk is about to happen. Within an hour there was our new baby, coming in a rush, blue and struggling to breathe as her small, glistening head emerged.

And then she stopped moving. The umbilical cord was looped around her neck and as she inched toward life, it tightened like a snare. I was pushed back from the bed as an emergency birthing crew came into the room and huddled over Maggie. They moved with practiced efficiency and I just stood there, dazed. Someone cut the cord and now the baby was untethered, not breathing, suspended between life and death.

"Now push," the midwife said calmly. "We want a big push. Everything you've got."

And just like that the baby slid into outstretched hands. She was taken away immediately, and it was only later the doctor told us how dangerous the moment was.

"If I had frozen, and she'd been stuck after the umbilical cord was cut, I don't know what would have happened," said Maggie.

No matter how natural childbirth is, each birth is astonishing; is a miracle. In past generations that baby would likely have died and the mother too. But moments after she came into the world breathless, the baby cried. She grasped life—swimming out of the darkness to join us, fighting and aloud. That was how Claire arrived.

And just like that I was the father of two girls: each perfect and brought into existence through an ancient biological process in which life and death are so close only a gasp separates them. There is one heart and then—announced by screams, tears, pain so savage women bite bed rails—there are two. Both times my head spun, my hands shook, and afterward I leaned against a wall for support.

Claire was brought back soon after the emergency birthing team had taken her away. She was clean and bundled, her blue skin now flushed pink, with a red mark around her neck where the umbilical cord had tightened. Maggie held her, smiling, looking down into a scrunched-up little face; holding her little hands.

"A perfect baby girl," she said.

"Two," I said.

———

I SMELLED MY BABIES, ran my nose across their cheeks, nuzzled in the soft curves of their necks; I kissed the tops of their heads and felt their hair, soft as dandelion thistles. I feared their fragility at first and cradled them in my arms afraid they would break. But they clung to me, slept with their heads against my shoulder. As they grew they reached up to be held and I rejoiced in carrying them everywhere, even when they grew so big it made my back hurt. And they grew so quickly, the years leaping ahead, vaulting over each other with bewildering speed. From carrying them everywhere to teaching them how to help me put up a tent

seemed to happen in a single summer. One day I was helping them walk, and the next, running after them as they
darted along the edge of a pond looking for tadpoles. One
day we were learning the words to "Twinkle Twinkle Little
Star," and the next we were lying on our backs looking up
at the night sky, and they were asking where stars came
from and how big the universe was. I marveled at their
curiosity, at their energy, at their interest in everything in
nature and their eagerness to join me doing anything outdoors. We canoed, hiked, and fished, shaping our changing
identities together.

Let's be clear. The bond a mother has with her baby is
forged at birth and grows beyond anything a father can
experience. The best a man can do is to be the second pillar.
Hold. Love unconditionally. Be there. Mothers give life.
Fathers give support. When I got it right I could feel my children's confidence growing, and that made me stronger.

"You have to be like the side of a swimming pool," said
Maggie's friend Lori, who had two boys a bit older than our
daughters. "Be there when they need to grab on. And when
they want to push off and swim alone, they will."

I listened and followed the advice as best I could, but I
knew the metaphor was flawed. It wasn't a contained pool;
it would overflow and one day they would slip over the
parapet, to swim away in the river beyond.

Before that I would try to teach them to read the water, to
know the natural world—and in the process I would come
to know myself better.

EASTER BLESSING

THE PATH TO THE RIVER led through a forest, and last night's rain dripped from the canopy. The floods of winter had risen months earlier, flattening undergrowth and leaving remnants of salmon, rags of gray skin, once silver and green, draped from low branches. It was a bewitching place and silent, except for the sound of water moving, drop by drop, from the treetops to the drenched forest floor. Ahead through the trees the surface of the river flickered with promise. My boots were quiet on the moss and I thought how silently a mountain lion could stalk here. It is probably not safe to go fishing alone on Vancouver Island, where there are more cougars per square mile than anywhere on Earth, but it is a good thing to do sometimes; it brings you closer to the forest, closer to yourself.

As I walked I thought about the beauty in my life, the richness the children had brought into it, but I pondered the darkness too. I had developed an increasing awareness of my own mortality, a growing fear of death which had emerged only with the birth of my children. To accept fatherhood is to acknowledge the transcendent importance of staying alive, not for your own sake but because of your responsibility and importance to others. But there was something else there too, a nagging, more distant, unfathomable feeling of despair that sometimes rose and subsided like a tide, as if my blood was pulled by the moon. In *Fly Fishing Through the Midlife Crisis*, Howell Raines wrote about the "black dog" of depression that followed him at times. I saw mine more as a wolf that trailed me through the forest, appearing when it wanted to.

In the surrounding woods, ravens called from somewhere in green towers. I looked up to see the highest branches were tangled in a soft gray mist, a tattered blanket thrown inland by the sea. And then on the trail ahead a hunched figure turned to face me. A great horned owl, awkward on the ground, lost without the wind beneath its silent wings, swiveled its head to place me in its field of binocular vision. Then it slowly turned to point its piercing yellow eyes at two ravens perched nearby.

"Look at this," it seemed to be saying to me.

It was a young owl, not accustomed to thuggery, that had been driven to the ground by the ravens, sullen and still, which were waiting for a chance to kill it. Black is perfect camouflage in a forest, and they looked like shadows waiting to fall. The ravens lowered their heads to look at me, calculating the game. I threw a stone and as it fell harmlessly in the brush they flew, clacking their strong beaks with indignation, dark robes flapping, to perch higher in a cedar. Seeing its chance, the owl lifted its wings and, with ponderous beats, rose above the ferns and swept off under the tree branches. I heard the ravens following, clattering from treetop to treetop. I knew they would bully and pursue the owl unless it could find a place to hide. After night fell it would be free, because owls fly easily in darkness but ravens do not. Such is the way of nature.

I was on the Tsable River, not bird-watching but looking for something rare: a steelhead on Easter weekend. The river was open for catch-and-release fishing then, but the next year, like many other rivers on Vancouver Island, it would be closed to angling because steelhead stocks had fallen to perilous levels. On the famed Gold River, once fished by Roderick Haig-Brown and his friend, and mine, Van Egan, the winter run of steelhead would fall to zero. I could sense the collapse coming; perhaps I'd sensed it was inevitable since that moment on the small stream in Sooke when the old man opened the car trunk to show me the brace of perfect, but dead, steelhead. He had killed a mated pair because he could—and because he, like many others, couldn't see the future.

I knew I had little chance of encountering a steelhead on the banks of the Tsable. The absence of fish from the valley was oppressive; it seemed to hang in the air like smoke from a distant fire. But I was searching anyway, fishing alone and hoping. I had left my young daughters at home because steelheading is a serious, demanding, obsessive business. You have to cover miles of water looking for steelhead, casting, wading from pool to pool, and, at four and eight, the girls were still too small for it. They would have found it hard to keep up, and having them trailing behind in a forest where mountain lions lived was not a danger I wanted to chance.

Emma was getting close to having the stamina to join me. She had discovered soccer, and playing in a mixed league against boys I could see her getting mentally and physically tougher. She would practice every night after school, running after the ball as I kicked it in the park across the street from our home. When it rained, she would go out alone, and I'd watch from the living room window while she splattered herself with mud. Claire was less physical and was happier mixing things in the kitchen with her mother. She was growing too, but I knew it would be years before I could take either of them steelheading. And as I walked to the Tsable that day I began to fear that by the time they were ready, the fish might be gone, might be extirpated not just from this river, but from all the rivers I knew.

Or maybe I'd be gone by then. Several old friends had died in recent years, two from sudden heart failures; a reminder of the fleeting nature of life, and the thought of my own mortality was a nagging presence. Still, I couldn't rush the girls into fly fishing. I'd have to first find a productive small stream for them to learn on, a place where they could begin to walk purposefully—but where they might also find their efforts rewarded by the urgent tug of a trout on the line. I wanted to find something like Penticton Creek, where they could experience the magic of fly fishing as I had. But I was still searching for that water, and the Tsable, with its steelhead run all but lost, clearly wasn't it.

In the meantime, I was working them up. A few days earlier we had sat together on a wharf, jigging hand lines baited with small pieces of clam. In the water below we watched surfperch mill around the hooks, nipping at the bait. The girls were on their hands and knees, leaning over the edge, watching the shiny fish flash in the sunlight and lifting whenever a perch bit.

"Pull now and you've got him," Emma said when she saw Claire's hook disappear into a fish's mouth. Claire stood up, lifting the small dancing fish, and Emma, who always took her role as the older sister seriously, caught the line and guided it to a red pail filled with seawater.

"There you go," she said, just as the fish wriggled free. It dropped into the bucket and darted about in confusion. Soon the girls had four fish, all bright silver with yellow stripes on their sides.

"They are a type of surfperch called shiners," I said.

"Will they bite me?" asked Emma, and when I said they wouldn't she gently lowered her hand into the bucket, trusting, but wanting to confirm the facts for herself. Claire put her fingers in too, laughing as the perch gently bumped against her. They watched the fish swimming in the pail for a few minutes, then tipped them back into the ocean with a cheer. Little fish first, I thought: shiners, then trout, then salmon. Steelhead, I hoped, would come eventually. That would be the last level to reach.

THERE IS A SPECIAL FEELING in going alone through a forest. The sense of being in nature is heightened and each step seems to reveal new miracles: the glow of sunlight through a leaf; the glistening trail of a slug; the tip of a fern curled tight like a baby's hand. Without the voices of others to distract me I went in silence through the woods and its beauty rained down. I was not singing or shouting to warn bears or cougars, not going in fear, but just moving, gently pushing aside the salal and slipping past the devil's club.

In his book on meditation, *Self and Environment*, Father Charles Brandt writes that if you are aware of your silence, you are not yet silent enough. And that is worth striving for. Charles, who I will write more about later, lived as a hermit priest on the Oyster River, where he contemplated nature, fly fished, and grew closer to God. As I made my way through the trees I forgot about trying to be quiet and I became a part of it all. All I could hear was the river ahead, flowing through the trees. The river drained the icy slopes of the Vancouver Island Ranges and flowed to the Strait of Georgia, murmuring all the way. It told the story of the forest and called home the fish that went to sea, offering salmon and steelhead a pathway to the mountains.

The forest was mostly second growth, but there were a few six-hundred-year-old cedars standing taller than the rest. The big trees had survived because they were growing in terrain too difficult for loggers, in gullies or on steep slopes, or else they were just missed. Maybe they got overlooked in a shift change. For whatever reason, when loggers had passed through seventy-five years earlier they left those trees standing on the fringe of the river flats. Outliers then, now they rose above all.

I stopped to look at them. Some of the cedars were massive. They had been mute for centuries and needed no lessons on silence. When I laid my hands against one, the bark felt layered by time. I could sense the roots spreading through the aqueous earth beneath us, drawing minerals from the soil, taking nitrogen and phosphorous from the decomposed bodies of salmon and passing it up to the tree's crown. High above, the tree's tip-top snagged a cloud. Behind the forest loomed mountain peaks loamed with spring snow, but in the lower valley it was warmer and rain soaked the greenness. Lining the riverbank were ancient, thick-trunked black cottonwoods that had been left uncut because their soft wood was of no value to loggers.

Ferns carpeted the forest floor, beading water on leaf tips that brushed against my chest waders. It felt like I was wading through the forest, like I was being painted by it. I came out of the woods flat washed and stepped knee-deep into the clear river. I stopped to knot a Black Doctor to my line. It was an Atlantic salmon fly, tied in Scotland, mauled by the teeth of a hook-nosed northern coho I caught the previous fall in the ocean off Vancouver Island. It is not a fly designed for Pacific salmon and is certainly not one known as a steelhead pattern—but I loved its elegant shape, topped by a swooping golden pheasant feather, and I liked the overall beauty of its body, which is wrapped with silver thread and lemon and black floss. When I opened the fly box that day it seemed to want to come out. I held the fly in my palm a moment, considering. It felt right.

"Today will be a good day," I said. The Black Doctor seemed to agree. I used a clinch knot to attach it, slipping the monofilament leader through the hook's eye, spinning the line back on itself, and wetting it in my mouth to ease the friction when I pulled it tight, feeling the barb close to my lips.

Bob Jones, a fly fisher, art critic, and outdoors writer who lived in nearby Courtenay, had told me when we talked earlier that year that "the Tsable comes on late," and that if I went there at Easter I should find fish holding in a big pool, below shale cliffs.

"If it hasn't changed up there, that is. And it does change a lot," said Bob. That was shortly before his death, before he became another old fisherman who the river will not see again. I missed his advice about writing and fishing, and going to the river, looking for his pool, was a way of paying respect, of remembering.

I found the rocky bluff he told me to scramble over, but the trail went straight up, through root tangles. Instead of following the difficult path he suggested, I chose to go across the river, wading deep on speckled stones. The water came up to my knees, my hips, my chest; it pressed against my lower rib cage, my lungs, my heart. I realized if one rock moved beneath my feet I'd go under. But the riverbed held firm and I made the crossing, water descending, streaming off my body with each step toward the far bank.

Upstream I found the deep elbow pool Bob had talked of. It seemed too slow to hold steelhead, but I swam the Black Doctor through anyway, searching for a fish. Upstream looked better, as it always does, so I wound in my line and went on.

I crossed the river, re-crossed, went through shallows, fished pocket water, searched behind tree trunks caught in the river and behind moss-covered boulders. It seemed as if I was fishing the forest as much as the river. In days past this place would have crackled with possibility. But as I studied the water I had faint hope that I might encounter a steelhead. I realized I was searching for something that had been lost. I was searching for a vanishing species, and I remembered the feeling I'd had as a boy when the old angler closed the car trunk and the steelhead disappeared in darkness.

———

ABOUT A MILE UPSTREAM I waded out to get past a tree that had fallen into the river, and in its shadow I saw a fish. A steelhead doe was holding in the water, barely moving. She had a tail the size of a dinner plate—translucent, spotted, powerful as an ocean tide. I could almost reach out and grasp her, but then she sensed me and with two quick tail beats she shot away, melting into emerald-green water.

Why hadn't I climbed over the tree on the bank and cast gently down? The current would have drifted my fly into the gloom, to the fish—and she would have taken the Black Doctor. Instead, I blundered and almost stepped on the fish, which fled for its life.

After that I tried to concentrate, hoping to find another steelhead, but a few pools later my attention wandered again, away from the river to the trees, to the traveling sky, to everything around me. On a sandbar I found bear tracks in fine sand. Beside the stream I picked up a roughskin newt curled on a rock, brown as a dead leaf. Turning it over I saw its belly was fluorescent orange. The gentle little newt protects itself by exuding a potent neurotoxin on its skin, and this glint of color was a warning to predators, a caution light flashing in the somber forest. I sat on a rock, the newt beside me. It made no effort to flee, and I put it on my knee. It looked up, curled its head and tail to show a blink of orange. It was spring and the newt was in search of a breeding pond. Throughout the forest other newts would be migrating as well. And on a cool spring day they would meet. I wondered if the lone steelhead I had seen would find a mate. Maybe there was a small run still, holding in a pool ahead.

Moving upstream, I reached a bend where the Tsable turned to meander down a new channel, leaving behind a dry bed that snaked through the woods. Following the path to nowhere I found a bluish-green pool set like a birthstone in a field of gravel raked clean by rain. I stood transfixed by the beauty, until wind shook the trees, leaves tipped, and drops of water spilled out, falling on my upturned face. I was awakened. The old channel led me back to the main river, where whole trees had been uprooted by winter floods. I did my best to fish under the logs, thinking of that missed steelhead and its huge translucent tail, fanning just beyond my reach. But the water was empty.

I came to a place where I could see plastic red survey tags hanging from the branches and a wide swath cut through the forest. At first I was afraid it was part of a new highway (please, not an off-ramp here), but reading a tag I learned it was marking a gas line right-of-way. A smaller evil, perhaps.

Above me I saw how the Tsable turned against a steep hillside, and by the way the mountain came down and caught the shadows, it looked like the river emerged from a deep canyon. I wanted to go up, to explore beyond the limits of what Bob had told me about, but it was getting late. So I turned back, stopping to eat an afternoon lunch where wolf tracks followed deer tracks across a sandbar, etching what appeared to be dance-step diagrams. The two-step promenade, the West Coast swing, the foxtrot: it was all there from the night before. No blood, so the dance hadn't ended badly. And on the edge of the bar, in soft sand, was one round, padded print. A cougar was with me. I touched the knife on my belt, and went on.

I cut off the Black Doctor and tied on a Black & Blue, a fly pattern originated by Van Egan, a friend, poet, and writer who lived and died on the Campbell River. Van and his wife, Maxine, fished often with their neighbor, Roderick Haig-Brown, and they shared a reverence for steelhead. One of the last times I visited Van we sat in his home, looking out at the Campbell, which flowed through his backyard, talking about writing and fishing. He drank Scotch and told me he would like to tie a steelhead fly for me, but old age had left his hands with tremors and he didn't think he could do a good job. He told me the pattern he had in mind, a Black & Blue, and I tied it myself later, but the fly he'd suggested couldn't conjure a fish from the depths of the Tsable for me. It was good company, though, and I felt Van was there, marveling at the river but shaking his head in sadness about all that had been lost.

Thinking of the old fishermen who were gone, I pondered my own life and thought of how fragile, how fleeting we all are, of how little time we have in nature. I thought of my young daughters, playing at home with their mother, and felt a shadow pass over me. I had almost been killed in a car crash once, had almost fallen off a cliff while fishing, had been stalked by bears and possibly cougars, and who knew when a heart might fail or disease might arrive?

I waited for the feeling to pass, a fleeting despair, then waded down close to where I spooked the steelhead earlier. After making a dozen careful casts to where I thought she was hiding, I swept my fly rod under the deadfall, hoping to flush the fish. I wanted to see her again, to confirm the miracle of her existence, even if it was just a flash of movement, a shadow under water. But she wasn't there and I felt my spirit sag, not because I didn't catch her but because steelhead were now so rare, so fleeting that even seeing one counted as an event and sometimes felt like a dream. It was like spotting a rare bird, and I realized steelhead might become like the ivory-billed woodpecker—the "Lord God Bird," as it was known because of the reaction people had when they saw it.

No one had seen an ivory-billed woodpecker since 1935 and the species was presumed extinct, but desperate, hopeful bird-watchers, the faithful, kept hope alive with their prayers.

I reeled in my line. It had been a long hike, with no fish taken, but a wondrous day, with the sun emerging late from behind ashen cloud. Not wasted time, for I had saved an owl and walked slowly where Roderick Haig-Brown, Van Egan, Bob Jones, and Father Brandt had all once fished. Perhaps that is enough, I thought.

———

THE DAY AFTER I FISHED ALONE on the Tsable was Easter Sunday. In the morning Emma and Claire searched through the garden for chocolate eggs, turning over leaves, crawling under bushes, searching in the forks of tree branches, and running back with full baskets. Emma, always practical and precise, counted the collection of eggs to ensure they had found them all. Then Claire, who never tired of magic, asked me to hide them again. After that I took them to walk up a small stream where I thought we might find a trout or two, but the water was empty, so we made small boats out of twigs and watched them float away.

"Where will the boats go?" asked Claire.

"Out to sea," answered Emma, thinking through the logical sequence in a very adult way.

"Like the owl and the pussy-cat in a pea-green boat," said Claire, tugging her older sister back into the magical realism of childhood.

"They sailed away, for a year and a day, to the land where the Bong-Tree grows," said Emma, reciting the poem by Edward Lear.

"They took some honey, and plenty of money, and then the owl and pussy-cat got married," said Claire, and they both laughed.

Later we went through the woods looking for a hidden pond I knew of. We found it, shining on the forest floor, with willows growing tight around.

"Look in the water," I said, as the girls peered through the branches.

"Salamanders!" said Emma, who on our walks always demanded to know the right names for plants, animals, and birds.

And there were. Dozens of them, hiding in the grass along the shore, floating just beneath the surface, with their black eyes blinking up at us. To submerge they pulled themselves under, like a child ducking under bedcovers. This was a breeding pond and the newts were converging.

"Roughskin newts," I said. "I found one just like it on the river yesterday. You don't see them together like this often."

The girls inched forward. Claire, who always believed in the good nature of wild things, picked one up first, and Emma followed. The newts curled in their hands, looked up, contemplating, fearless, inquisitive. When the girls released them, they swam through the clear water with gentle undulations, as if they were dancing.

There had been no trout for the girls, no steelhead for me, but in this small pond we saw the resurrection of nature taking place, so it was an Easter blessing nonetheless.

WHERE THE
RIVER LEADS

IT WAS MIDSUMMER IN the dry British Columbia interior, where a great forest, ravaged by years of fires and logging, sprawled over dry mountains. I awoke in a farmhouse near Salmon Arm where Maggie's parents—Don, an engineer who served with the Canadian army in Germany during World War II and ran paper mills afterward, and Nora, a cheerful, practical woman who raised their seven children—had retired to an old house surrounded by orchards and fields. We were lucky to have the farm as an escape from the city, and Emma and Claire, both brimming with a curiosity about nature, loved it when we visited. There was a big garden where they helped their grandma pick vegetables, and a tractor their grandad would take them for rides on, letting them balance on his knees, with their small hands gripping the vibrating steering wheel.

Lying in bed we could hear a flicker drumming on a pole in the garden. The girls were in a makeshift bed on the floor, but when I looked over I saw they were both wide awake, listening to the sound, whispering as to what it might be.

"It's a bird," I said. "The farm alarm clock." In a moment they were up and down the stairs to the kitchen, where Nora would serve them porridge after taking them outside to pick fresh raspberries. Maggie smiled and turned over to go back to sleep, but I got up, feeling a need to be on the water and wondering where I might go. The farm was a busy place for the girls and they loved to trail along behind their grandparents, helping in all the chores, never being told they were in the way. For Maggie and me it was a respite from our hectic lives in the city, where we had staggered our newsroom schedules so that one of us was always home when the girls weren't at daycare or school. I was lucky to have a journalism job I enjoyed, but since the girls had come into my life I'd increasingly seen work as something that took time away from being with my children. My father had dedicated himself to his profession, often coming home late at night or not at all, and I didn't want to follow that path. It was clear to me that in the end, looking back, the job would mean little, but the children would mean everything. Making breakfast for Emma and Claire, cleaning food off my tie before I left for the office, rushing home in time to see a piano recital or watch them in a school play, and struggling with all their questions ("Why do we have money? Why do birds fly? What are stars made of? Who is God?") left little free time. Not that I wanted it much, because I sensed how fast life was moving, how rapidly they were growing, and didn't want to miss any of it. But sometimes I did need to slip away to the water, for the silence, the contemplation.

At breakfast I told the girls I was going off to explore a nearby stream, to see if it might be a good place I could take them fishing later, and they didn't object. They knew I always came back from the water happy. And they were already making plans for the day anyway.

"Gramps says I can help get honey," said Emma, who would fearlessly stand next to the hive while bees swarmed around the netting draped over her head. "And we can feed the cows," said Claire, who knew the neighbor's cattle, with big, soft, slobbery noses, would come to the fence to take grass or sweet apples from her hands. These were such simple activities, but for city children there was pure joy in life on the farm. I remembered my own childhood, surrounded by nature, raising wild ducks and collecting chicken eggs. The girls weren't hunting in the forest as I did as a boy, but I knew their grandma would take them for long walks in the woods, and she'd let them run free, with her dog bounding beside them. They would see rabbits and maybe flying squirrels. Later, in art classes at school, images of trees, animals, water, and fish would emerge, in dominant colors of blues and greens.

———

WHILE THE GIRLS PICKED FLOWERS and tomatoes with their grandparents, I put my fishing gear in the truck and went in search of trout in a small stream I had never fished before. It ran down a valley close to the farm. Don had fished and hunted as a young man and in his home office there was a rack of shotguns, a battered metal tackle box filled with pike lures, and a collection of old casting rods and reels. But he had set aside those activities in retirement and knew nothing about the local fishing.

I had crossed over the Salmon River on the highway bridge several times and thought it might do as a fishing spot for the girls, but I was uncertain because it flowed through open fields where the water was mostly without shade. In the summer heat it might be lifeless. And none of the fly fishers I knew had ever mentioned the Salmon River, which suggested it could be one of those watersheds where the fishing had been ruined. I would go to see.

It was quiet driving down the valley, the truck feeling empty without children laughing and squabbling in the back seat. But fishing alone is not lonely, no more than praying in a church is. It was a chance for me to concentrate on my fly casting skills and to get in touch with who I was before I became defined by fatherhood. And I wanted to explore the river. When I was young the rivers in British Columbia were full of trout and salmon and steelhead. I could go anywhere then and catch fish. But by the time my daughters were born, many streams were desolate, with stocks devastated by overfishing, by logging, or by the withdrawal of water to irrigate hay crops, and I didn't want to take them to a place like that. I knew some streams still held trout, and I wanted to know if the Salmon River had survived; if it still had magic.

THE TOWN OF SALMON ARM is named for the great runs of sockeye that once flooded up the South Thompson River and migrated into Shuswap Lake. From the lake the fish head up tributaries, such as the Adams River and the much smaller Salmon River. The Adams is world famous for its big salmon runs, and there are pathways and viewing platforms along the river so that tourists can marvel at the sight of spawning fish. There is none of that on the Salmon River, which once was just as rich in sockeye as the Adams.

In 1905 sockeye flooded up the Salmon River in such numbers that a fisheries officer described how the water level rose, lifting his boat, when a massive school of fish moved into the stream from the lake. The water heaved up off their backs, creating a high tide of fish. The river had lots of big trout then too, which feasted on the salmon eggs, so plentiful they drifted out of the overflowing nests and rolled along the bottom, and on the fry that emerged in swarms in the spring. But then the settlers came. They cleared the forests on the flats along the river, and with the shade removed, the water heated up in the summer. Baby salmon struggled to survive. Spawning salmon were considered so expendable they were netted and pitchforked out of the river to fertilize farm fields. Nature was plundered to grow hay. And farther down the watershed, near the ocean, commercial fishing fleets killed salmon by the millions. Logging ruined fish habitat. Cattle beat paths to the river, causing siltation, stockyards leaked manure into the stream, and corn farms sucked out millions of gallons of water to irrigate crops.

According to what I'd been able to read by the time I arrived, searching for a legacy for my daughters, the Salmon River had a small run of salmon left, a trickle where there had once been a flood. But I couldn't find any information about its trout fishing. I hoped I might find a deep pool somewhere, where I could show the girls how a trout will come up for a dry fly.

I pulled off the road into a patch of dust near a bridge and got out to peer into the water. The sunlight was harsh and I felt the heat crackling over my skin. I thought about global warming, and worried about the planet my daughters were inheriting, but when I put my hand into the water of the stream I felt better. It was cool and alive.

I slipped into the shade of the bridge and put my rod together while pondering options. The first thing to consider when you prepare to try a new river is fundamentally this: do you fish upstream or down? Downstream from the bridge the river ran under a bower of willows. It looked inviting, but tight, with water slipping away from the glare of the sun under a dark-green arch. It was like the stream Richard Brautigan describes in *Trout Fishing in America,* with shadowy water running through a "long tunnel of telephone booths." I thought it hopeful that while telephone booths had pretty much gone extinct since Brautigan wrote that, in 1967, trout were still around.

Upstream from where I stood the river was fast and shallow, running between hayfields where the water was exposed to sunlight pouring down, through 94 million miles of space. Past the hayfields the river banked off the base of a black cliff, and that was as far as I could see. There was no good trout-holding water in sight upstream, and no shade—not a single telephone booth of it—but I decided to fish up anyway, because it always seems more interesting to find out where a stream comes from. And I already knew where it went: back down through the farmland to a summer lake filled with speeding boats and water-skiers. Also, it looked less productive for trout upstream, the water too open, too warm, so it might not have been fished by anyone.

There was a certain delicate pleasure to be had in rigging up a fly rod under the secrecy of a bridge. Cars hissed past overhead, tires squelching the melting tarmac, while underneath, surrounded by the gurgle of the brook and the smell of oiled wood, I secretly contemplated a selection of tiny trout flies. I had one box of flies, two extra leaders, a line clipper, two sandwiches wrapped in wax paper, and water in a plastic bottle tucked in a canvas shoulder bag. The fly rod was green with silver wrappings; it weighed three ounces, had a polished burl wood reel seat, and was destined to be given to one of my daughters. I didn't know which girl would get it, but it was a beautiful Sage rod and I wanted it to go on fishing after I've gone.

———

THE WATER OF THE SALMON RIVER was cool around my legs. I waited until the road above was quiet, then started upstream, not running but wading quickly, hoping to get out of sight around the corner before any traffic came by. You don't want too many people seeing you setting off with a rod, otherwise they might follow, bringing cans of worms, portable stereos, and the family dog. It's happened.

At the bend the river grew deeper and the road was out of sight. The water was dark blue-green at the base of the cliff. An old cottonwood, its bark as rough as an elephant's skin, lay in the water near the tail of the run. Its root wad was torn partially from the bank; its branches trailed downstream, the current rippling through it like wind. In the field nearby I heard grasshoppers rasping hind legs against hard, dry fore-wings, which vibrated like cellos. I listened, thinking how my daughters would enjoy this: the summer concert. Sometimes insects flew out of the grass with a cracking sound and I heard them hitting the ground as they landed. Some fell in the water. As they struggled, trying to kick back into the air, they sent concentric rings across the surface.

I tied on a fly to mimic a grasshopper; it had brown turkey-feather wings and a yellow wool body, and looked real enough to jump out of my hand. It was big and a bit clumsy at the end of my line. When cast, it hit the surface with a loud splat, just as real grasshoppers do.

The fly drifted alongside the cottonwood, then was gone in a perfect, bright swirl. The rod went up and the trout went down into the blue-green waters. The graphite rod thrummed in the heat.

I realized at that moment how much I liked the quiet sounds the world made, away from traffic and people. It chirped, clicked, rustled, and splashed. Standing in the water I felt as if I had been made lighter. I felt like I fit in, as if I was tied with a blood knot to the river.

The trout, when it came splashing to hand, seemed crafted by a jeweler, with a band of pink along its lateral line and an emerald-green back splattered with dark spots. Its body was cold and polished, perfectly calibrated to the stream. The barbless hook slipped out from between its small, sharp white teeth, and in a twinkling the fish was gone, back to its hiding place.

Whenever I release trout I think of my daughters and the generations of anglers to come. I hope that the progeny of the fish I let go will one day rise to their flies, will dance across the water for them, will turn, flashing colors, in their hands.

I kept wading upstream. Kept catching fish every few casts. With each one I drew a little closer to the river, learning its secrets, and I wondered how many others had fished here. The abandon with which the trout came to my fly suggested they hadn't been caught before.

I fished slowly and got lost in being part of it all. At the head of one pool I stood in the middle of the river, waiting for a trout to rise. I'd seen it moments before take an insect from the surface and knew it would come again. One more rise and I would be able to mark the trout's location and drop my fly in exactly the right spot. With nowhere to go but back downstream to the traffic, I was patient. I waited; barely breathing, not moving, concentrating on the water, watching for the trout. When the fish rose again, dimpling the surface, I lifted my rod quickly to cast—and there was an explosion of water behind me. I jerked around and saw a two-point buck leap out of the river in panic. The deer made the bank in one bound and went crashing off through the brush, leaving me behind, heart pounding, hands shaking a bit. After a few minutes I went looking for another fish.

The farmland soon gave way to forest, with big trees leaning over the river. The water was noticeably colder in the shade. Sitting on a log, eating lunch, legs dangling in the stream, I watched a man come around the bend upstream and begin wading toward me. He wore a battered cowboy hat, a plaid shirt with its sleeves torn off, and blue jeans that were wet to the knees. He carried a long wooden spear ending in a trident of black, pointed steel, the outer tines curving in slightly. Best fishing outfit he could think of, I supposed.

He saw me, nodded, waded across the stream, and sat down.

"Fishing?" he asked.

"Yep. You?"

"Yep," he said, leaning his spear against the log.

I offered him a sandwich, realizing I'd packed two, and he accepted it as if he'd expected it.

He told me he was Secwépemc and was fishing for salmon in his home stream. His handmade spear was for killing Chinook that came from the Pacific, up the Fraser River, through Hells Gate, up the Thompson River through a stretch of white water called the Big Gulp, up the South Thompson River, across Shuswap Lake, and finally into the small, diminished Salmon River, his home stream, where we sat.

"The run is due just about now," he said.

He was interested in my fly rod and flies. Never fished for trout himself, he said. The Chinook weighed twenty pounds in this river and the trout came in ounces.

"They like to hide under the logjams," he said of the big salmon. "It's cooler there, I guess. I feel for them. Let the current kind of move the spear shaft around 'til you bump into them, then you raise it and..." He finished his story with a sharp jab, and I could feel the spear sinking into the firm orange flesh of the Chinook: a gift from the sea to the Secwépemc.

"Pretty big fish, sometimes they pull me in, right off the log," he said with a laugh.

He was coming back to fish the river for the first time in ten years, he said. Why had he been away so long?

"Incarcerated," he answered. I didn't ask why, but you gotta do something pretty bad to do ten years in a Canadian jail. Murder probably, I thought.

We talked about how the valley had changed in his lifetime, with farmers cutting down trees to grow hay crops, forest fires ravaging the mountains, and loggers clearcutting everything they could. He said the river was smaller, warmer, less wild than when he was a boy, and he wondered how much more the salmon could take.

"Will our kids and their kids be able to fish here?" he asked, expressing a fear I felt myself. He shook his head to say no, or maybe to say he didn't know the answer.

"People gotta change, or we'll lose the salmon," he said. "Too many people thinking only about money."

He asked me about fly fishing and was interested to hear how trout come up from the bottom of the stream to grab a fly that looks like a grasshopper. I put a fly in his hand and he smiled.

"Looks real," he said. "That is amazing."

I learned about spearing salmon, about how the vibrations he feels through the wooden spear shaft tell him how big the fish are and which way they are turning.

"I can't believe you can get twenty-pound salmon in here," I said. "I thought a twelve-inch trout was big."

He held my fly rod and laughed at how delicate it was, shaking it gently. It weighed less than his cowboy hat.

"I can't believe you can cast with that," he said.

"The rod is graphite, like the stuff they use on the Space Shuttle," I said, and he looked up, and me too, as if we expected to see something coming out of the sky.

I told him I was surprised the trout fishing was so good.

"Not big fish," I said. "But there are rainbows in every pool and they are easy to catch."

He nodded, like saying he approved, like: *good to know.*

"Well, nobody fishes trout here. You know this is Indian land," he said. "White folks don't come here and the Indians just fish for salmon."

I said I didn't know I was trespassing, and should have looked at a map because I did know there were Secwépemc reserves in the valley.

"It's okay. No harm done," he said. "Nice sandwich."

He didn't ask me to leave, but when he started downstream, I went with him. We waded together and he looked under logs for any sign of salmon.

"Watch out for bears," he said. "There's really a lot. They know when the salmon are coming and start to hang out." He remembered this from before prison. I got ahead of him, wading on when he stopped to probe under a big logjam, sweeping the spear into the darkness, hoping for the bump of a Chinook.

We were near where I had spooked the deer earlier, and just then I saw something moving in the tall grass along the riverbank. I stood still and waited for the buck to come out. The chest-high grass waved as the deer came toward the river. It was heading right for where I stood in the water, and I smiled. I thought: I won't move and I'll see how close it comes this time.

Then the grass parted and a big, ginger-colored bear stepped out. He was so close I could have made one false cast and put a fly on his back. His fur was glowing in the sunlight. When we saw each other, I jumped back, splashing like a trout floundering to get unhooked. The bear, forgetting for a moment that his feet were still moving, tumbled off the steep bank, landed on his head, did a somersault, and came up running fast, sending rocks rattling all along the gravel bar. Behind me the native guy let out a whoop. He never saw anything like that in prison.

"Woooo-ooo!" he yelled. "Run, bear, run!"

My heart was going so fast all I could hear after his yell faded was the blood pounding in my head. I waited for the spear fisher to catch up. "That was fun," he said, and we waded down together for a few minutes, looking for the bear, which had vanished like an apparition.

As we walked in the stream, the Secwépemc spear fisher told me how everything was changing, how the river had shifted in its bed, eating deep into the cliff. The bank had caved in where his uncle's fishing cabin had once been.

"It was here," he said. We were looking at an empty, grassy bank that was slumping into the stream. There was no sign of the place where he'd grown up, and learned to fish. The smile he'd had when the bear ran away was gone and he looked bereft now, like someone confused, or in mourning. Floodwaters had taken everything away. I imagined somewhere in a logjam downstream there might be floorboards, with salmon finning underneath, or a sunken cookstove, with trout drifting in and out of the oven.

The Secwépemc man stood and looked at the empty space where the cabin used to be, where his childhood used to be. He was silent, forlorn. Perhaps the nothingness that was there now reminded him of the ten-year hole the prison sentence had left in his life, of the things he'd lost that would never return, of the salmon runs he'd missed. Memories of his life were strewn by floodwaters and scattered through the river.

"I turn back here," he said. "We are at the edge of the reserve."

He looked downstream. Once all the land was Secwépemc and all the water held salmon.

"Gotta believe the Chinook are coming," he said. "Maybe tomorrow. Maybe next week."

I wondered. In the decade he'd been away Chinook stocks had fallen throughout the entire watershed. Maybe twenty-pound Chinook were just a memory in the Salmon River now, like his uncle's cabin, like the steelhead in the home stream I'd had as a boy.

"Well, I know there are still trout here, at least. I will bring my daughters to catch some," I said.

"Good thing to do," he said. "My father wasn't around for me, but my grandfather taught me to fish." He looked again for the cabin that wasn't there. Then we shook hands in the middle of the river.

I sloshed down through the flats, where the water was shallow and fast, and looked back after a moment only to see that he'd vanished. The Secwépemc spirit man, like the deer and the running bear, like his grandfather's cabin, was just gone.

By the time I got back to the truck it was getting toward evening, cooling as the Earth turned away from the sun. It was as if the shade hidden under the bridge had spilled out.

ALL SOME PEOPLE WANT TO KNOW ABOUT when you go fishing is, how many did you catch? Any big ones?

Fishing's not about that; it's about going where the river takes you. It's about singing grasshoppers, jumping deer, and bears doing flips. It's about the movement of planets and the befriending of strangers. It's about seeing the diminishment of nature, and understanding the loss. I had had a good day trout fishing, but the Secwépemc salmon fisher had caught nothing. As I put my gear away I knew I had witnessed a tragedy.

When I got back to the farm my daughters were in the tangled garden with their grandmother. They came running to the truck carrying fresh-picked flowers that blew in the wind.

"We got honey from the hive and grandpa got stung," said Emma.

"I fed the cows and got slimed," said Claire.

Their skin was brown, their hair golden from the sun, their eyes so bright and alive. I told them I saw a bear do a somersault and met a native fisherman with a spear. Their eyes were big, imagining how exciting that was. They wanted to go fishing there as soon as they could, but I told them I would have to find a different place for them.

"That was Secwépemc water, and I didn't know I wasn't allowed to be there," I said.

"It's their special place?" asked Emma.

"Yes," I said, "and guarded by spirits, so I won't trespass there again."

I searched other sections of the Salmon River after that but never found water as good as I had that day, and never did take the girls fishing there. I knew I would have to keep searching for a stream for them.

———

LATER THAT SUMMER I WENT to Penticton Creek, returning more than three decades after I'd moved away as a boy. I went back to the creek with mixed emotions, feeling some nostalgic excitement, but trepidation too. Surely it would all be changed, the way the Salmon River was for the Secwépemc spear fisher. My daughters were then about the age I'd been when I first explored the creek as a boy. And on my return I was about the age my parents were when our family settled in the big house in the orchard. I didn't know what that coincidence meant about the continuum of lives and how trout streams echo through generations, but it felt like it meant something.

I wondered if this could become a learning stream for my daughters, as it had been for me. Or was that too much to hope for? I had been lucky enough to grow up next to streams that I got to know, that I claimed as my own. If you have a home stream you have a reference point in nature, a benchmark against which you can measure change and time. You know the stream's moods through the seasons, you know the movement of its fish, and that connection moves in you like a tide. In spring when I hear the geese flying north I know the lakes where the rainbow trout will be rising to flies, and when the peaches start to grow ripe I know the streams where pink salmon are running. I remember the times I have gone there, the friends I have fished with. Growing up in the city meant Emma and Claire were largely disconnected from the seasonal rounds, and I wanted to find streams, lakes, rivers that would bind them to the land; that would give them memories.

I drove through Penticton, found the road to the upper bench, and went searching for my old family home. There, somewhere, surrounded by a sea of apple trees, was where I had lived in such simple happiness and where my parents had still shared a dream of raising a big family together. Now my mother was living alone on Salt Spring Island, where she went for long nature walks, and my father was remarried and had another son, giving me a much younger half-brother, Nicolas. My four other brothers, who I had walked to school with through the orchards, were scattered widely—Jon still at sea fishing, Tim and Andy living in the Yukon, Steve working in the Canadian Arctic. As I searched for our old family home I heard the faint echoes of their voices, calling on me to play catch, or daring me to climb higher in a tree. Somewhere here we had picked wild asparagus together along rock fence lines, on the mountain above we had prodded rattlesnakes with sticks, and in the nearby creek we had caught small trout with our hands.

I stopped on the road where the driveway used to be, but I couldn't see the redwoods that once towered above the orchard and marked the entrance to the yard. I couldn't find the giant old apricot tree that shaded the back door. It was all gone, taken by the floods of time, the trees knocked down along with the old house that had been built in a time when furniture was delivered from England by sailing ships. All of it swept aside to make way for a modern subdivision of ranchers and bungalows.

I drove into a cul-de-sac that had replaced a grove of cherry trees, turned onto a road where thickets of willows had once flourished, and found the creek. At least that was still there. But it was sad to see how houses and lawns had spread along the stream bank, replacing the tangled bush. I thought, this is not where I want my daughters to learn fly fishing. I want somewhere wilder. But as I walked upstream I recognized the old pools, cradled still in the bends of the creek. The internal framework of the stream hadn't changed, even if the land around it had.

Given the state of the world, I didn't expect to find the trout where they once had been, and from the walking path I looked down into empty pools. The water seemed darker; harder to penetrate. But as I walked I wondered if, just maybe, there could still be a few speckled brook trout in the water I had fished so many years earlier as a boy. Could the progeny of that great fish I lost in the headwaters be here?

I was carrying a fly a rod so expensive I wouldn't have believed as a kid I'd ever possess one, but I was unsure I would use it now. Could I just be inviting disappointment? If I caught nothing it would be another blow, another reminder of how things were slipping away. But I wanted to at least wade into the stream of my youth. I stepped off the bank, and when I did the water felt cool and familiar folding around my legs.

Across the creek from where I stood there had once been wild woods. Now there was a retirement village of bungalows, and in one I saw a man standing in his living room, watching me through a picture window. He lifted a glass of white wine in salute. I touched my hat, looking to him, I suppose, like a Victorian portrait of an angler in a trout stream, not like a man in search of his past.

"You're not actually going to fish there?" asked a bemused resident who stopped behind me on the streamside path.

"Thought I might," I said. "I fished here as a boy. Forty years ago almost. Before there were any houses."

"Well, good for you," he said. "Nobody ever fishes here now."

Then he walked on. I looked up and the drinking man had left his living room. So I was alone on the stream in a way that could not really pass for solitude, but which, for the moment, would have to do.

I thought of the little boy, the bobber and worm, the fragment of glass in the dark hole. And of the great fish I had once lost in the headwaters.

When I knotted on a size 16 Adams, a tiny dry fly I had tied with prim, upright wings, I had to slide my glasses down my nose to see the line. I had weaker eyes than I did as a boy, and maybe that's why I couldn't see the fish. Or maybe they just weren't there. Gone like my old home in the orchard. Like the Secwépemc cabin on the Salmon.

I waded deeper, false casting as I went, to get within range of a deep slot. I imagined a red-and-white bobber tracing the current seam, pausing to dip and spin, signaling a nibble, where the trout should be holding.

The first cast fell lightly on the surface and I mended the line, softly throwing a loop upstream so the fly drifted naturally. A fish came up almost immediately, its glossy back breaking the surface as it went down with the fly. I lifted gently, set the small hook, and landed the trout after a short tussle. I released it and took a fish with my second cast, then with my third. They were six inches, much smaller than the twelve-inch trout I used to catch. But they were still beautiful, with bright red and blue spots and wormlike markings on their green backs. These were my boyhood trout, and it was as if I had opened a dusty jewelry box and found a family heirloom. One fought much harder than the rest and was close to a foot long. I held it gently against my leg, then lifted it above the surface for a moment to let the light play on its flanks. I remembered those colors.

"Wow," said the man who stopped to watch as he returned from his walk on the path. "That's a keeper!" He said he was going to run home to get his rod and his wife, and soon they both started fishing in the pool above, casting on the stream where the willows had been replaced by housing and where many people had forgotten the beauty that lies within Penticton Creek.

Later, just before darkness fell, I drove through suburbs, walked to the dam, and climbed the rock face to the fence. I looked across the reservoir, to the valley the creek ran from. Up there, around a few bends, was the pool and the memory of a great fish I'd found in the headwaters.

Posted along the reservoir were signs warning it was illegal to trespass, just as there had been when I was a boy. But I knew kids were still sneaking in, yielding to the call of the forbidden water, because there was a hole in the fence, right where I remembered it.

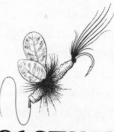

CASTING INSTRUCTIONS

EVERY SUMMER MAGGIE AND I took our daughters camping. We pitched our tent on lakeshores and beside streams and rivers. Before I taught Emma and Claire how to cast I showed them how to lie on a dock and peer through the cracks to see trout finning below. I helped them turn over rocks on the lakeshore to find caddis larvae, wandering aquatic insects that carry on their backs intricate homes made of tiny sticks or stones. I taught the girls that adult caddis look like small moths and that when they skitter over the surface to lay their eggs, trout chase them, striking with abandon. This changed the way they looked at lakes. I showed them dragonfly nymphs clambering up the stems of bulrushes to shed their shells.

"When you see dragonflies zooming about over the lake, you know there will be nymphs underwater nearby," I said. "Trout love to feed on them." I took a newly emerged dragonfly off a bulrush and brought it into the canoe.

"They look fierce, but won't bite if you don't hold them roughly," I said as Claire watched the insect resting on the gunwale, testing its new wings. Tentatively she laid her hand down and waited while it clambered onto her fingers. With its tendril wings gingerly unfolding, its ferocious mandible gasping harmlessly, it gently clasped her skin with tiny, clinging feet. She held it in front of her face, turning it in the light, and Emma found one too and it sparkled blue.

The girls learned to differentiate dragonflies from damselflies by the way the insects held their transparent wings (a dragonfly's wings extend from either side; a damselfly folds its wings like a tent over its back), and they marveled at how the sunlight glowed through the glossy filaments. They blew on the unfolding wings to dry them, then laughed as the insects lifted up and soared away like sparks on the wind. Later, they chose dragonfly nymphs from my fly box and we fished slowly over weed beds, the girls alert for a strike because they knew the fish and the insects were interwoven in the water.

They saw nature and felt it. We drifted under soporific skies. Heard the calls of ravens, a sonorous *glop, glop* echoing in the forest, and the ripping sound of air through pinion feathers as ducks tilted in to land on the water near us. Emma collected hawk feathers, consulted with her mother to identify them correctly, and tucked them under the band on my fishing hat. "Red-tail," she said. "Wing feathers."

Claire brought me a mountain bluebird, found dead by a roadside, its ruffled warm body painted the color of van Gogh's *The Starry Night*. She held it gently, but not sadly. She had grown to understand that life is fleeting and nature had its own rules.

"How do you think it died?" she asked. We inspected it. There were no cuts, but its neck was limp.

"Maybe it hit a car. Maybe that peregrine we saw fly over earlier struck it," I said. She nodded. I took a few semiplume feathers for us to tie flies with and set the bird back in the forest. The next morning it was gone, because the forest is always hungry, but a mayfly imitation with greyish-blue wings soon came to rest in my fly box.

One day the three of us stopped fishing on a lake when the girls spotted a gosling, flopping on a grassy point nearby.

"It's in trouble," said Claire.

We went ashore and saw it was tangled in fishing line. I threw my jacket over the struggling bird and held it while the girls, tender and determined, unwound the monofilament from its wings and legs. When they released the gosling it ran across the water, splashing its small, downy wings to gain traction, racing to rejoin the flock waiting in a nervous gaggle. The adult geese craned their long necks and called urgently as the gosling dashed toward them. Emma and Claire cheered. Then the girls went along the shore, picking up all the bits of lost fishing line they could find so it couldn't trap any more birds. All of this was as important as the fishing, which at first the girls did just by holding the rod while letting the fly troll slowly behind the boat. Learning how to cast came later.

———

OF ALL THE WAYS TO cast a line, fly fishing is the most complicated, obfuscating, and elegant. The mechanics of a functional cast are simple enough, but a good cast takes exact timing, and getting it right takes practice. Done well a cast is effortless, meditative; the line is propelled across the sky and the weightless fly, alive with movement and light, falls like a single drop of rain. Done poorly a cast ends in a jumble of line and a frustrating tangle.

Emma and Claire had a lot to learn, because fly casting and fly fishing are not the same thing. But I knew once they understood the fundamentals of how to cast well, they would enjoy their days on the water, because a good cast is like a prayer—full of hope.

When the girls were big enough to wield a nine-foot fly rod I felt it was time for them to take the next step, and learn how to cast. They watched me demonstrate the movement on the grass. In place of a fly I tied a small piece of white cloth on the end of the line, so they couldn't hook themselves.

"Imagine you are standing with your back to a barn door," I told them, repeating a lesson that had helped teach me the proper technique. "Drive your rod up on the back cast, but don't let it hit the barn door. Turn your head to watch the line unfold, and the moment it straightens out behind you, throw it forward."

They watched me cast. Thought about it for a moment, then took turns lifting the rod and throwing the line. They both looked back, to keep the rod tip from hitting the barn door.

I tossed Emma's orange baseball hat out on the grass and told them to try to hit it. The casting motion became automatic as they concentrated on the target, and soon the little white tag was darting back and forth and drifting down like a mayfly to land near the cap.

"If you can cast like that with this heavy, old fiberglass rod of mine, you will be deadly when you get a new, light rod," I said.

After they mastered the cast with the antiquated Hardy rod that I'd had since I was a teenager, I trusted them with my much lighter, and expensive, Sage, made of graphite.

Several weeks after her first lesson, Emma broke into a smile when she cast with the new rod, which uncoiled with a snap, accelerating the line in a way she hadn't imagined.

"Oh, that casts nice!" she said, standing in a boat and shooting the line over the water. It was spring and we were on a trout lake, with fish swirling on the surface as they chased caddis flies. Emma aimed her casts toward the ripples on the surface, and after an hour of trying finally connected with a rainbow trout that jumped in the air with her fly in its mouth. She let out a whoop, and I knew then I would give her that rod one day, when the time was right. I think she knew that too.

———

A GIFTED ROD IS A wonderful thing to have, because a fly rod is as much a talisman as it is a tool. When you fish with it, you fish with the love of whoever gave it to you. It becomes infused with memories of the waters you fish and the big trout and salmon you encounter. Sometimes just holding a rod can bring those memories alive and make you want to go fishing.

I have a split cane rod built by Peter McVey, a former boxer and master chef who immigrated to Canada from England in the 1960s and who lived, until his death in 2019, in Merritt, near some of the finest trout-fishing lakes in the world. I once visited Peter in his workshop, and we talked about fishing for big Thompson River steelhead and Kamloops trout in lakes while he worked on a new rod. I told him I wanted to get a small rod like that someday to fish for small trout in small streams.

"Yes, I know how much fun that can be," he said with a big smile. "You really need a little three-weight rod for that."

I didn't know then the rod he was building in his shed was for me. Maggie later gave it to me as a birthday present. When I first took that bamboo fly rod out of its wooden case I was struck by its beauty. It was small and light and strong, made by a boxer with the hands of an artist, and when I lifted it, it trembled, like a gun dog does when it scents a game bird.

On the Skagit River that summer I fished with it for the first time, delicately casting a tiny Adams dry fly. Before I had worked my way through the first pool of the day a rainbow trout came up and plucked the fly from the surface. The three-weight rod bent to the cork handle, and the fourteen-inch trout seemed much bigger than it was.

For Emma and Claire, that small rod was a revelation. It was so light in their hands and it cast so beautifully. We fished the Skagit together, sharing the bamboo rod that Peter had made just for that river. And walking back to the truck at the end of the day, Emma carried my light graphite rod and Claire carried the tiny bamboo rod. I had them walk in front, in case a cougar came from behind, and as we walked the girls sang songs, whistled, and shouted to anything that might be on the trail ahead.

"Hey bear!" they called every now and then.

They only caught a few fish that day, but it was enough, and they were passing through the forest in joy. We walked through shadows and sunlight, the girls feeling good to have fly rods to carry and happy to have the sound of the river nearby.

That night we slept in a tent close to the stream and I lay awake at night until they were both asleep, just listening to the forest, planning where we would fish the next day.

Whenever I think of the Skagit now I think of Peter McVey, who died suddenly from cancer. He left a beautiful rod behind, a tiny sliver of the universe, and he would have smiled to see the girls fishing with it that summer's day.

CLAIRE GOT HER OWN ROD and reel one Christmas. She peeled off the wrapping paper and slid it from its case, laughing because she had grown up enough to have her own gear. No more hand-me-down stuff. No more shared-with-sister stuff. This was hers to fish with when she wanted. It would rest in her room, with her fishing vest and fly box, and would go out on the water when she chose.

"A rod that you trust always fishes better," I told my daughters.

It didn't take long for Claire's new rod to be christened, and soon she had complete faith in it. One evening on a trout lake near Kamloops, she tied a strike indicator and a fly known as a Pumpkin Head on her line. She threw it thirty feet, making an easy, lazy cast, then she sat on the bottom of the boat, her back against the stern seat, using her life jacket as a cushion. She got a book out to read. A breeze made the strike indicator bob up and down on the surface, and a few feet below, the little green fly with an orange bead for a head picked up the movement.

"You have a fish," I said a few minutes later, as her strike indicator dipped under the surface. Claire lifted her rod, which was lying across her lap, and a trout went dashing across the lake, stripping line off her reel. She got to her knees, then stood to fight the trout back to the net. She caught two more trout that way, outfishing me by letting the rod and the fly and the wind do the work.

"The Zen of fishing," she said to explain her technique. She had blind faith that her rod was lucky—and it was.

———

EMMA BONDED WITH HER ROD, which was then still mine, on a trip we took to Haida Gwaii. My friend Harvey guided us through a deep forest, draped with moss, down a steep gulley that opened suddenly before us, to the banks of a fast, clear river. We could see the salmon moving in the shadows under logjams. But the banks were a tangle of vegetation and any kind of cast was impossible.

We made our way upstream along steep, slippery banks, until we found a waterfall with a roaring plunge pool. The backs of salmon showed here and there, cleaving the bright surface. Emma waded out, roll casting because there was no room to lift the line behind her, and a big coho slashed at her fly on the first cast. She fought the fish briefly, and lost it. The battle stirred the other salmon and they slunk deep in the pool.

I joined her for a while, but the fish were too nervous to strike. I quit, but Emma kept casting, her fly probing the water, her patience allowing the pattern to slip deeper into the pool. She was feeling her way toward the fish, the rod tip moving to trace the path of the drift. It was like watching a conductor moving her baton over the orchestra, waiting for just the right moment to gesture for the violinists to play. I sat on the bank with Harvey, watching her work the water.

"She's really got it," said Harvey. "She's just a master with that rod."

Then it bent in a deep arc. When the fish shook its powerful head, Emma's arms jerked. The salmon and the angler were joined in that instant; it was as if an electrical current was running up the line, going through the rod, and being conducted into her body.

The salmon raced across the water, spun into the air, and dove into the foam at the base of the falls. Downstream were logjams where the fish could easily have found freedom by tangling the line in roots. But instead of running out of the pool the salmon stayed and fought beneath the waterfall, deep in the ancient forest. And Emma, silent and determined, hung on. The rod shook and the line hummed like a tight wire. When I got up to help land the fish, Harvey touched my elbow.

"Wait," he said.

All too often protective parents step in to shield their children from failure, from setbacks, from disappointment. I once grabbed Claire around the waist when she was standing on the rolling deck of a boat playing a big salmon at sea. Later it wasn't the feeling of fighting that large fish she remembered, but how I had held her so tightly, not trusting her to keep her footing. It was my nervousness that she remembered, not her own joy.

So Harvey and I watched Emma bring the fish in alone. It was a big salmon, but it was being defeated by the untiring resistance of the rod, which dipped and absorbed each pull.

Emma backed to shore, stumbling a bit, and then, sitting in the shallows, she pulled the salmon against her waders. It lay still, and she took her forceps and twisted the hook free. With two tail beats the salmon was gone.

"I love this rod," said Emma, holding it up in the forest light. So I gave it to her.

With their own rods the girls became skilled casters and could soon throw their flies pretty much anywhere they wanted to. But I could see they still had things to learn about fishing, about understanding the behavior of fish and about where they might hold in a stream. I had spent hours peering out from the willow bushes on Penticton Creek, studying the currents and the movement of brook trout. In the process I had learned that fish usually appear as abstract patterns that are impossible to decipher in the water, and that often the only way to find them is to look for their shadows. You read the water to tell where a fish is most likely to be holding in the current, and then you focus until you see the unseen. I knew a small stream was the best way to teach them that. I was still searching for the right water, for the perfect place.

CATCH AND RELEASE

WE WERE STAYING THAT SUMMER with family, and I had seen the stream from the highway bridge. It was just a short drive from the house we were at, and one day I stopped at the crossing. Below the bridge the stream ran into a lake, next to a beach that was crowded with swimmers and running children. Upstream didn't look promising either. It had been channelized, with its natural twisting course straightened so that it would not overflow its banks and flood the adjacent orchards.

The creek ran quick and shallow through the channel, and I couldn't see any trout-holding water. There were no corner pools because there were no corners. But as I was about to turn away, I looked farther up and felt some hope. The stream emerged from a canyon, and beyond that were mountains clad with pine forest, which meant the headwaters must be wild. Later I drove into the hills, tracing the blue line on the map and stopping when the road drew close to it. Then I walked along a trail. When I came to the stream

I found an old man, sitting on the shoreline with his boot heels in the water, a bait-casting rod in his hands.

"Hi," I said. He looked up and nodded a greeting, apparently unsurprised to meet a stranger in the middle of nowhere.

"Can you help me get up?" he said. "I sat down and now I'm stuck. Being old sucks."

He wore a greasy baseball cap, a faded blue shirt, jeans, and battered old work boots, the leather wet from the stream. His face, beneath white stubble, was tanned, and years of squinting into sunlight had left deep wrinkles at the corners of his eyes. I took his arm and he mine. He was heavy, had rough hands, fingers stained by tobacco, and a firm grip. I could tell he had once had a powerful build. He didn't come up on the first try. But on the second heave he made it to his feet, rocking slightly before he took the stance of a fighter, as if braced against a world that wanted to knock him down.

"Catching any fish?" I asked.

He answered by nodding to the grassy bank and a small bag made from the leg of a pair of blue jeans. The bag was soaked, and when I picked it up I felt the fish inside, slippery and smooth. Out spilled three lovely rainbow trout.

"Used to get big ones here," he said. "Now ten inches is good."

I said I was looking for a place to take my daughters fishing.

"Upstream," he said. "This is as far as I can make it now. But upstream is better. That's where I used to go, when I was younger."

I asked him if he needed help walking.

"No, I'll be okay. Truck's not far," he said, although I hadn't seen any other vehicle parked on the road. I went farther along the trail and saw how the stream lay cool in the shade of the forest. It looked encouraging. When I turned back a few minutes later the old man was gone. He had just vanished, and I wondered if I had met a friendly, shape-shifting water spirit. Perhaps he had come to give me a glimpse of myself twenty years in the future, so infirm from old age I needed someone to help me stand next to a trout stream. I felt some comfort in knowing my daughters would be there for me when that time came.

———

THE SOUND OF THE STREAM flowed through my dreams that night and the next day Claire and I headed up Stoney Creek on our bikes, riding past where the old man had rested. The stream was often out of sight, so we were listening as much as watching for a place to fish. At first the brook came fast out of the mountains, crashing boulder to boulder. It was too turbulent to hold fish, so we kept going until the water grew quieter. We left our bikes and went down the hill, trying not to slip on the slick duff of ponderosa pine needles blanketing the ground.

"Now that looks nice," I said when we glimpsed a pool through the trees. It was calm and deep with a cathedral train of bubbles winding across the dark surface. The stream made a dogleg turn under a logjam, creating a perfect place for trout to hide on a hot day.

We waded through the shallow, fast water above the pool and stood on a gravel bar. Claire was eleven. She was tall, elegant, and her inner thoughts were an increasing mystery to me, but she hadn't reached an age yet where being with her friends was all that mattered. That time would come, but as she strung up her rod she seemed happy to be on an outing with her father. We looked in her fly box, considering all the possibilities, and after a moment she pulled out a small, gray dry fly that had barred, upright wings.

"An Adams," I said. "Good choice." I knew it would ride high on the surface, so she'd be able to track it on the water. "It looks like a mayfly, like a mosquito, like a lot of little insects," I said. "And it is one of my favorite flies."

"I know," she said. "I think I watched you tie this one."

She knotted it on the leader and looked at the pool, pondering where to begin. Claire had caught trout in lakes, but streams are different, more challenging, and she was still learning about them. Moving water is complex, enigmatic, and difficult to read. The rippled surface hides the location of fish, and the flow requires you to constantly watch your fly and the line, so they move at the same speed. If they get out of sync, the fly will drag unnaturally and trout will turn away.

But streams are a joy to fish because they are more intimate than lakes. They saturate the air with the sound of moving water and reflected light. And to fish them you have to wade. In warm weather you don't wear waders, just boots and blue jeans or shorts, wading wet and letting the sun dry you. You follow a stream up or down and can't see very far ahead, so each bend brings a surprise. Sometimes you will find a beaver pond hidden in the forest, or a fresh bear track in the mud, or an unexpected deep pool where trout have collected like gold nuggets. Sometimes a big fish will flash out of the darkness. Following a stream is a revelation, a journey through nature, and that day I hoped Claire would find in the moving water of Stoney Creek the magic I had found as a boy on Penticton Creek.

For a few minutes we stood quietly and watched how the flecks of foam drifted with the current. It made the water easier to read, tracing it out for us.

"The fish will be hiding under the logs, but there is no room for a back cast," I said. "So just roll cast your fly diagonally across the stream and let the current carry it down."

She looked at the bower of branches over the stream behind us, saw how a back cast would get tangled, and nodded as she thought through the movement her rod would have to make. Her first cast was a bit sloppy, but as she lifted her line to try again there was a sudden splash behind the fly.

"Oh!" she said.

"You missed one," I said. "Put your fly right back there."

She did, with a quick forward flick of the rod, and a rainbow took, darting up from the bottom to grab the Adams.

She brought the trout in, skittering across the surface, and once it was in her hands I showed her how to quiet it by turning it over. Trout are never upside down in the water, and when you flip them on their backs they often lie completely still, bewildered. The tiny hook was barely pricking the trout's jaw, and I plucked it loose. She turned the fish right side up and tipped it back into the stream, laughing as it darted off.

"Does it hurt them?" she asked. It wasn't a question I had pondered much. As a boy I was concerned only with the chase, but I knew I had to think about it now.

Neurobiologists and fish researchers agree that fish feel pain, but are divided on just what that means. I couldn't give Claire a definitive, science-based answer, so I relied on the anecdotal; on the experience I'd had in my lifetime of handling a thousand fish, of feeling their cold weight and sensing their tremulations through my fingertips.

"I don't think a fly hook usually does hurt or damage them much, because their mouths are so tough and bony," I said. "One day I was fishing up north when I hooked a pike. It fought for a minute, then cut the line with its teeth. The friend I was with cast, there was a big splash, and he hooked the fish I'd just lost. When he landed it, my lure was dangling out one side of its mouth and his was on the other. If my lure had hurt that fish, I don't think it would have grabbed his. We let that pike go, and I got my lure back."

I told her I also once caught a big cutthroat that had a distinctive scar on its flank. Ten minutes after I released that fish, I caught it again on the same fly. Pain triggers avoidance, but neither that trout nor the pike showed any aversion to lures that had been hooked in their jaws only minutes earlier.

I have often seen examples of fish that seem to be pain free, despite significant injuries. I have landed salmon that struck my fly even though they had fresh wounds left by seal attacks. And a friend caught a trout shortly after it had been dropped by an osprey. Those fish swam away after being released.

"When you see stuff like that, it is hard to believe fish feel pain or experience trauma the way we do," I said to Claire. "And certainly the sting of a hook is nothing compared to being bitten by a seal, or torn by osprey talons."

I also reminded her of the day I was released myself. I had paddled down a lake with Claire and Emma to fish an evening rise at a creek mouth when a gust of wind drove my line off course as I made a forward cast. I felt the fly sink into the back of my neck. I couldn't pull it free, so I asked Emma to take my forceps and grasp the shank of the hook.

"Just do it as if you were releasing a fish," I said.

Without hesitating she gripped the fly, locking the forceps. "Got it," she said, and with a quick tug, the hook came out.

"Did that hurt?" she asked.

"Didn't feel much," I said, a small trickle of blood running down my neck.

"Catch and release," she said, and we went back to fishing.

Humans are far more sensitive than fish, but I had hooked myself in a tough layer of skin just above my shirt collar without any suffering. Though I can't know with certainty, I can only hope it is like that for trout.

"Fish fight," I told Claire, "not because your hook is hurting them, but because the resistance of the line alarms them. It triggers a flight response and they race for cover in an instinctive reaction. If you relax the tension on a line, just let it go loose, hooked fish will often stop fighting."

I also told her fish don't experience fear as we know it.

"I sat on a viewing platform for days once and watched as bears ran through the shallows, trying to catch salmon," I said. "The fish darted into hiding whenever a bear chased them. But the moment the bear left, the salmon went right back to what they were doing, as if nothing had happened. If you were chased by a bear, you would be in shock, but fish are different from us. Sure, they experience stress fighting to get unhooked. But all their lives they are fleeing predators; escaping loons, bears, and otters without any apparent trauma. So it is hard to believe tugging on a line is damaging. If you play and release a fish carefully, I don't think you do any lasting harm—physically, or emotionally."

I told her that catch-and-release fishing was an old concept, dating back in angling literature to 1828, when Sir Humphry Davy, an English chemist famous for discovering several elements (and inventing the miner's safety lamp) wrote *Salmonia: Or Days of Fly Fishing*. In that early book on the delights of sports fishing, he states that "every good angler, as soon as his fish is landed, either destroys his life immediately, if he is wanted for food, or returns him into the water."

But catch-and-release fishing didn't really start to take hold, at least in North America, until the 1930s, when two writers promoted it as an important conservation measure.

"Roderick Haig-Brown in Canada and Lee Wulff in the US really popularized it," I said to Claire. "At the time, trout and Atlantic salmon stocks were declining in many areas, while the number of sports fishers was growing. They pushed the idea that anglers should release at least some of their catch. Over the years it became widely practiced, in many places it became the law, and now a lot of people let *almost everything* go. Indigenous people oppose it—they say we are playing with our food. But if sports anglers killed everything they caught, they'd empty the streams of fish. This way we get to fish, and the fish get to live and reproduce."

I wasn't sure if I had convinced her or not. I hoped maybe the fish might do that.

AS CLAIRE FISHED ON STONEY CREEK that day I sat under the shade of the pines, watching. Almost every cast drew a splashy rise, and soon she had caught six trout, carefully releasing them all. Then the pool grew quiet, and she came to sit with me.

"Those fish are so beautiful," she said.

We listened to the stream running through the forest for a few minutes, just looking at the sunlight on the water.

"Let's explore downstream," I said. "See what we can find."

We skirted the logjam and went down, wading carefully, casting into the small pools that formed behind boulders. Patterns of light and shade shifted on the water, and every now and then a trout would pluck a fly from the surface. We took turns catching and releasing fish.

On one corner the creek cut deeply under a towering rock face. It looked promising, and Claire made a perfect cast, but nothing came out of the shadows for the Adams.

"They are back, too deep under the cut to see your fly," I said. Claire opened her fly box and switched to a Gold Ribbed Hare's Ear, which imitates an insect in its nymph stage. Aquatic insects move about in streams mostly by crawling, but sometimes they are dislodged or they just let go in order to change locations. Drifting with the current, they become exposed and vulnerable. That's when trout feed on them, snatching them out of the current the way a bird will intercept a flying insect.

Claire pinched a small split shot weight on the line above the fly to make it sink. With the weight it was more difficult to cast, but she could swing the rig out and drop it into the water, letting the current carry the fly.

"This is how I used to fish as a boy," I said of the swing-and-drop method, thinking of the big trout I'd lost on Penticton Creek when I was about her age. "Except I used a worm instead of a fly."

She dropped the nymph in the fast water at the head of the pool and fed out line as it drifted down. The fly disappeared under the rock shelf, and the little weight bumped on the bottom with a ticking sensation picked up by the rod tip.

A sudden pull came from back in the darkness. This was a bigger fish, and her rod bent down like a dowsing stick urgently finding groundwater.

An unseen trout always seems much larger than it is, so we were watching for the first glimpse. And after a moment there it was, a flash of silver deep in the grotto. The trout was struggling to stay under the shelter of the rock, to stay in the fish cave where it had lain in wait while insects drifted into its mouth.

But then the trout yielded and came racing out, dashing across the shallows, before it turned and tried to regain its lair. Claire held it with steady pressure on the line, then got its head above the surface and skidded it to her feet in the shallows. The trout lay still while we admired it.

"Twelve inches," I said, a trophy for a stream where most fish we had caught were only eight inches.

She released it and waded back into the darting water at the head of the pool, her rod held aloft in her right hand, a coil of loose line in her left. The weight swung back and then went forward, pulling loose line from her hand and dropping into the water, into my past, into the hidden cave where the trout moved among a steady drift of bright, shining air bubbles, pine needles, aquatic vegetation, and insects. This was not elegant casting, but it was effective, and more importantly it required that Claire understand how everything was moving: the current, the food entrained within it. She had to read the water to find the trout.

The Hare's Ear nymph drifted so naturally it seemed alive, and another trout soon took. The rod jumped. It was another big fish. She brought it to shore and released it. On the next cast there was a violent strike, a brief struggle with a fish that seemed larger than the others. Then it was over. Claire looked up, her shoulders sagging when the line went slack. The trout was off. After that she made several more casts, drifting her fly through the pool without a take, and we knew she had caught all the fish, or perhaps they were hiding deeper in the stream cave, where she couldn't reach.

"That's it," she said. We looked up to see the sun had moved behind the mountain. She clipped the fly from her leader, slipped the split shot off, and reeled in the line. We followed a dusty deer trail up a steep bank away from the stream, loose rocks rattling down behind us, and stepped over thatches of cactus as we went through the shaded forest to find our bikes. Riding away from the stream we stopped to watch a red-tailed hawk passing high above, a limp snake dangling from its talons like a piece of garden hose. "It's going to feed its young," I said to Claire, and soon we heard chicks squealing in their nest back in the forest.

When we got home Claire didn't boast about her good luck to her sister, who'd chosen that day to go swimming at the lake.

"Got some nice ones," was all she said. "Lovely stream."

EARLY IN THEIR FLY FISHING LESSONS I taught both my daughters to squeeze down the barbs on their flies so they could easily release fish. I taught them how to use forceps to take out hooks. And for the first few years that we fished that's what they did—they landed fish, and let them go.

"The ultimate experience in fly fishing is not in hooking a fish, but in holding it," I told them. "It is only when you have a wild fish in your hands that you see its true beauty. And that's mainly why I fish, for that moment."

There is something about physical contact with another living creature that is always amazing. I recalled that when I first held Emma and Claire it took my breath away. I don't mean to compare holding an infant to holding a cold-blooded trout, but when you take something living in your hands, when you ponder the miracle, when you see its sacredness, it can trigger a sense of wonder that is profound.

The first time Emma let a fish go, she looked up, water dripping from empty hands that had just cradled a trout, and gave me a look of pure joy. "Amazing," she said.

That summer day on Stoney Creek, Claire had the same experience, and laughed in delight. She had shown me she knew how to handle fish with respect, how to release them unharmed, and now it was time for the next lesson. I had to show her how to harvest what she caught.

This wasn't something I did lightly. It is a delicate balance to teach your children how to love fish—and how to kill them. But both are part of the art of fishing and living in nature.

———

A FEW DAYS LATER I returned to Stoney Creek with Claire and her younger cousin, Laurel, with plans to bring home what we caught. Nervous about how the lesson might go, I took the first trout Claire drew from the water that morning, and carried it up onto the bank. I showed the girls a spot on the trout's head, just slightly behind and above its eyes.

"Its brain is smaller than a pea," I said, clasping the trout in my left hand. "If you strike it in the right place, the fish will die instantly and without pain."

I took a stick and knocked the small trout on the head. It quivered. And lay still. Then I washed it and laid it in the grass.

"I don't like to kill fish," I said. "But I do like to eat them. This is the cleanest, freshest food you will ever get: a wild trout, taken from nature. And I think it is honorable to harvest your own fish, rather than getting someone to do it for you."

Laurel, who had fished before with her father and had seen fish killed, wasn't bothered. But Claire was expressionless, pondering what she'd just witnessed, and I couldn't tell if what I had done had upset her or not. Some of the fish we caught that day were let go, but I said we needed enough for a meal. And so we harvested four. I killed three and Laurel one, but Claire chose not to. Her face was inscrutable as she watched us dispatch the trout. I gutted the fish and we picked wild mint along the stream edge, stuffing the trout with wet leaves. Later we fried the trout in butter, with a wedge of lemon squeezed over the tender, white flesh. The taste of mint lingered, and Claire smiled at the praise when her mom and aunt tasted what she and Laurel had caught, prepared, and cooked. It would not be too much to say that meal was reverential.

———

LATER THAT FALL, ON A LAKE where we were catching lots of big trout, I killed a fish Claire landed, and Emma dispatched her own catch, delivering a clinical, swift blow, just as I'd taught her. I told my daughters I wanted them to clean their fish this time. Claire had flinched at the killing, but she was not squeamish about taking a knife at the dockside table and splitting the trout up its belly. She slid out the internal organs and ran her thumb down the backbone to remove the long skein of blood collected there. She was interested in how the trout was made and looked at the gill filaments with curiosity. This was how the trout drew oxygen from the water; it was what allowed the fish to inhabit a world mysterious to us.

Emma was studious about the evisceration process and precise in her movements. She made a smooth cut, the blade parting the firm white skin on the belly to reveal bright orange flesh underneath. She opened the cavity with her fingers, examining the intestines and the gill filaments before pulling them out with a twist.

"Is this the stomach?" she asked, probing a bulge in the gut pile with her knifepoint.

"Yes."

"Let's see what it was eating," she said, slicing open the cartilaginous tissue. We squeezed out the dark, mushy contents and mixed the soft, wet, pulp with a few drops of water to separate the mass.

"Chironomids," I said as small, black things, each the size and shape of a comma, became distinct in the murky soup. "Tiny insects, like mosquito larvae. Hundreds of them."

Claire looked at her trout on the cleaning table.

"What's that?" she asked, after cleaving the stomach of her trout and diluting the contents as Emma had done.

"Little shrimp. Or scuds, some people call them."

"He was stuffed with them and still wanted our fly. Greedy," she said stirring the trout's last meal, which included dozens of small shrimp.

"Yes. Trout feed instinctively—and when they get a chance to feast, they do," I said.

A few of the shrimp were still alive, clenching and opening their bodies in an attempt to swim. Claire cupped them in her hand and returned them to the lake, where they darted off into the weeds. I could tell she was contemplating the matrix of nature, the interlacing of life and death. To feed, the trout had killed harmless shrimp and diaphanous chironomids, and we had killed harmless trout so that we, in turn, could feed on the fish.

"I don't know if I can bring myself to kill a fish yet," said Claire. "But I think it is good to harvest some. Not too many. But some."

I nodded in understanding.

"Killing should not be an easy thing to do. And you should never do it without some remorse and without offering thanks," I said.

We washed the blood off our hands at the fish cleaning table, and I felt that my lessons had resonated with Claire and Emma, that both now saw harvesting wild fish is being a part of nature. The line ran through us, through the fish, through the insects, through the plants in the lake, and that bound us to the sun that poured light upon the water and stirred the wind. We had just killed two beautiful trout, but we hadn't entirely removed them from the food web. Rather, we had become a deeper part of it through them. And the transition would be complete when we ate the flesh of the fish.

The girls carried their rainbow trout up to the cabin proudly. We had a meal to make.

CAUGHT

FROM THE START AS I guided my daughters toward a fly fishing life, I hoped they would grasp the meditative nature of the sport. I knew if they did, they would be hooked on the experience of it all and wouldn't need to catch fish to have a good day afield.

So we made campfires, studied wild game tracks in the mud, listened to grouse drumming in the bush—a percussive thrumming that seemed to be inside our heads—and saw hawks fall like stones on their prey. We heard wolves howl back at us from across lakes and watched loons swim under our canoe, dark, fibrillating shadows suddenly there, then gone in a ripple of water. We swam in rivers and when fall came, we watched bears chase spawning salmon. And sometimes we concentrated on catching fish, but that was a small part of it all.

Not everyone who fly fishes feels this way, immersed in nature; many are simply in pursuit of trophies, or big numbers of fish caught. When I first began fishing I felt something was wrong if I went home without a catch to show off. The term commonly used by anglers to describe a fishless outing is "getting skunked," as if it is so shameful it stinks. My initial measure of success was to catch a fish, then to catch more and bigger fish. But after I picked up a fly rod I began to feel differently. I came to understand that catching fish had little to do with the joy that came from simply being out there, not thinking, just moving and being part of it all. I wanted my daughters to get to that point too, to realize that while they were on the water to search for trout or salmon, they were really there for much more than that. They were there to feel nature unfolding around them. They were there to walk the road to nowhere and everywhere.

Fly fishing is about the way light reflects off falling rain; it is about the way the clatter of yellow-headed blackbirds can signal an insect hatch, and the way a lake grows dark underneath you as thunderclouds come over the mountains above. And if you can see that and feel it, there is happiness just in being on the water.

That's the seed I tried to plant, and I waited for signs. But of course I knew that to get there, they would have to catch fish too, just as I did. The fish would pull them through to the bigger experience that lay beyond.

————

EMMA QUICKLY BECAME A SKILLED CASTER, but her transformation into a real fly fisher came in stages. The salmon she caught on a fishing trip to Haida Gwaii had been a big step. But there was more to come.

One summer we went fishing on a small stream in the Canadian Rockies. As I searched through my fly box, Emma wandered upstream alone. When I came around the bend a few minutes later she was on her knees in the water, holding a three-pound cutthroat against her waders. Its vivid red gills flashed as it gulped water. She held it just the way

I'd taught her, one hand gripping the fish above the tail, the other cradling the front part of its body, just behind and under the pectoral fins. When she opened her hands the fish swam away, disappearing like a piece of glass into translucent green water.

"It took my dry fly," she said, as if describing something that couldn't possibly have really happened. She kept ahead of me after that, wading upstream, casting into riffles and behind logjams, taking one westslope cutthroat after another. Most were eighteen inches long and some even bigger. They came up from the pebbled bottom and turned down on her fly, and she found and fought them without my help or advice.

Later we sat on a high grassy bank, eating lunch with the stream shining beneath our feet. Mountains soared above, and as we watched the water a big trout came out to feed on floating insects. The trout materialized, tilted up to the surface, slurped a mayfly, and slowly vanished; synchronicity as beautiful and as calibrated as planets turning in space. When it sank, its camouflaged back dissolved into the river bottom. Its inky spots became the shadows between the rocks, its green back became water—and just like that it was gone.

"Did you see it?" Emma asked.

I slipped into the water and cast to where we thought the fish was, but it stayed hidden. When I climbed back up on the bank the fish began feeding again. Emma laughed. We watched the trout rematerializing and then disappearing as it plucked insects from the surface, dimpling the reflected image of the snowy mountains, wavering in the current, trembling.

"This is so great," said Emma.

We walked all day along that stream, stopping to look at grizzly bear, wolf, and elk tracks, catching big fish, and sometimes scaring trout with our clumsiness.

Every cast was a self-taught lesson, and I never had to offer my observations. If Emma did everything right the fly would settle to the surface gently, would drift naturally with the current, and a trout would rise to take it. A sloppy cast, a dragged fly, or a shadow falling suddenly across a pool would startle a trout and it would vanish. You learn from that. Step by step. Cast by cast.

The forest and the sky and the mountains surrounded us as we moved from pool to pool. Coming back to the truck late in the afternoon we pulled off our waders and took our rods apart. I knew that fly fishing was part of her now and that though other things would demand time in her life, she would always remember the trout stream in the Rocky Mountains.

ONE SUMMER WE FLEW DEEP into northern British Columbia, to a lake surrounded by such vast wilderness that for an hour we looked down from our floatplane and didn't see any sign of human activity: no roads, no power lines. Just a great forest and now and then a glimpse of all the life that it contained: wild rivers, ragged white mountain goats on black cliffs, a moose surging out of a lake, a bear and her cubs, turning rocks high on a scree slope.

We were with two other families, making a small camp in a clearing on the shore of a mountain lake that held big rainbow trout. The lake was on a high plateau. A rough, gray mountain peak stood to the south, and across the water far to the west was a distant, snowy range, illuminated, then cast in silhouette by the setting sun. To the north and east lay an undulating, undisturbed forest of pine and spruce. After the sun went down the lake glowed, as if it was releasing light back into the sky.

Standing at the campfire, with sparks spiraling toward the faint, emerging stars, I could see a cedar canoe anchored off a nearby point, an elegant swoop of green on a wild canvas of black and blue. I knew it was tethered to the soft, weedy bottom of the lake by a stretch of yellow rope tied to a rock. There was an almost imperceptible offshore breeze. Not enough to ruffle the surface, but persistent enough that the anchor line was pulled tight, as if the canoe was trying to drift with a tide into the night sky.

A young woman with a fly rod stood to cast her line over a patch of water tinged green from a bed of weeds growing in lime-rich mud in the shallows.

I watched as my daughter slowly retrieved her line and then threw it out again, far over the water. Emma had been casting all day, ashore only for a quick lunch, and seemed oblivious to the oceanic darkness rising around her. I knew why. Over that shallow point earlier in the day she had cast a big, black leech pattern made of rabbit fur, leaning into the cast and ducking as the heavy fly shot past her head. Drawing the fly back along the drop-off, retrieving it slowly so that it swam through the water with a waving motion, she felt a violent pull. A rainbow trout, possibly one of the eighteen-pounders the lake held, yanked the rod tip into the water. The butt of the rod kicked into her stomach and the line went tight as a great weight surged into the depths. Straining against it she felt the cork handle twisting in her hand as the trout fought.

Fly fishing is a visceral experience, where sight and sound and light are all stimulants, but it is the sense of touch that is most electrifying. The rod vibrates when a fish accelerates, it jerks when a fish shakes its head; it transmits heaviness from the sluggish weight of weeds gathering on the line, and then a sudden slackness signals that a hook has lost its hold—or the line has broken.

Emma had been startled by the power of the big fish, the biggest trout she'd ever hooked, and watched amazed as the line sliced across the flats, hissing as it cut the surface.

It is hard to guess the weight of a fish that is unseen in the depths. They can feel much bigger than they are, but this one jumped once, up high, coming down heavy. It was one of the great fish we knew the lake held. A hunter, a top predator, had come in from the depths to cruise over the weed bed, and now it was racing away trying to shake the leech caught in its jaws.

Emma just hung on, hoping it would slow before she was spooled, before the line was stripped completely from the violently spinning reel. Then the trout changed direction and there was a slow, wet drag on the line as the fish ran through a weed bed. The weight built up as weeds accumulated on the line, and then the fish was gone, the line slack and lifeless in an empty lake.

And she couldn't quite believe it: not then, not hours later.

So she was back, anchored in the same place over the luminous marl bed, triangulating her canoe's position with a tall tree, the tents, and a mountain. She was trying to reconnect, searching with hundreds of casts, buoyed by the hope that the trout just might be there. Again. Maybe. Maybe. Maybe.

She had caught some big trout of five pounds, but wanted one of the giants that prowled the lake. We'd flown high into the mountains just to have a chance at such large trout, after all. As I watched her cast, my eyes slowly filling with the night, I realized after a childhood spent traipsing around with me to countless lakes and frog ponds, she had become a true fly fisher. She was still a teenager, but after fishing for surfperch on oily docks or for small trout in cold, windblown lakes where blackflies swarmed us and bears left tracks in the mud along the shore, after waking in tents to listen to owls call in the lonely darkness, and hearing billions of crickets shrilling along a desert river, a big trout had raced off into the dark water with her heart.

She was caught now, as I had been as a boy, by the loss of a great fish.

That night she came in pleased with the trout she'd landed, including one that jumped over the canoe, forcing her to duck, but still shaking her head in wonder at the huge rainbow that got away.

"A slab," she called it.

Her younger sister, Claire, had fished with her through part of the day on the mountain lake, but hadn't lost a trophy and was happy working around the campfire, helping to make dinner. For her fly fishing was mostly still just a means to be with people she loved in the outdoors. Though she was always happy to go out on the water with me, catching fish just didn't seem that important to her. I realized that maybe she didn't need to catch fish because she'd had success early and that gave her the feeling that fish were out there, just waiting for her.

On a summer day a few years earlier, while we were staying in a cabin on a small lake, I left Claire with Maggie as I readied a rented rowboat that was too small for three. While Emma and I fussed with our tackle, Claire lay down on the dock and peered through the wooden planks. And there beneath her a secret world opened. Several big trout were finning below. As we rowed away, Claire stood up, took her rod, and flipped out a fly, getting it to drift into the shadows, into the hidden world she'd discovered.

A pair of fishermen outfitted in expensive fly fishing rods, fishing vests with multiple pockets, and baseball caps that declared their loyalty to Orvis, a high-end tackle manufacturer, were coming in.

"Nothing," said one of them as our boats passed. He held his hands up as if to say the fishing gods had abandoned them.

Just then Claire's rod bent deeply. A rainbow trout leaped between the two boats and landed with a splash before dashing back under the wharf. Claire held on. The fish pulled the rod tip into the water and bent it under the wharf, then jumped on the other side of the dock.

Claire was looking down into the water in front of her, and the trout was thrashing the surface behind her. There was a lot of confusion as all the men started shouting advice at once and Maggie and Emma cheered.

"Hooray!" shouted Emma.

Claire swung her rod tip around the end of the wharf so she was facing the trout, and she refused to yield. By the time I scrambled back onto the dock, the trout was splashing in the water below her feet. I dipped the net in and lifted a four-pound rainbow trout; big by anyone's standards. The two anglers who had just circumnavigated the lake looked dejected.

"We didn't get a bite all morning," said one, pushing back his Orvis ball cap.

I pulled out the fly and Claire held the fish gently, then released it. She looked amazed as it bolted free. She has always fished with serenity because of that day, knowing that a big fish will come to her when it will.

―――

ON OUR LAST NIGHT ON the mountain lake a pack of wolves began to howl. The girls listened, wide eyed, and then Claire howled back. After a moment the wolves answered, curious, excited, questioning the high sweet voice calling to them in the gathering darkness. Emma joined in and the girls and the wolves sang to each other, then the forest grew silent.

FLY
TYING SPELLS

EMMA AND CLAIRE SOON LEARNED that there is something magical about being on a beach when salmon are running past within casting range, or on the water when trout are rising to a hatch. They had come to know about the amazing beauty of fish because they had held them. And they had embraced the rituals of fly fishing: the vestments, the prayers, the sacrifice.

But to take them deeper I decided I needed also to teach them how to tie flies, how to make by their own hands, with twists of thread on a hook shank, imitations of insects and small fish.

Catching a fish on a cast fly is a remarkable experience. But a fisher moves to a higher level of understanding when they catch a fish with a fly they have made themselves, whether it is something they have spun out of their imagination, or have tied by strictly following the prescriptions set out in scriptures by the masters. There are hundreds of instructional books to choose from, but one favorite of mine is *The Fly-Tying Bible*, by Peter Gathercole, and I used it to guide my daughters into the obscure, dark art.

———

SITTING AT MY FLY TYING VICE I tied a Mickey Finn, a simple, impressionistic fly pattern that evokes a minnow and is a good place for a beginner to start. I looked at it critically, holding it up next to an illustration in a fly tying book. It wasn't perfect, so I used a sharp edge, cut the material off the hook, and tried again. Claire and Emma watched and waited for their turn at the vice. When I got it right I tied two identical flies and put them in a box.

With their nimble fingers, Claire and Emma made nice work of the flies they tied. Sitting at their elbow I gently prodded them if they were about to miss a step. In tying flies, the material has to be put on in layers and in a prescribed order, so the fly can be tied off neatly at the end, with all the components in the right place. Forget a step and you have to either unwind it all, or cut the material from the hook, and start over. We advanced from easy to more difficult flies, from big hairwing patterns like the Mickey Finn, which are about as long as an adult's index finger, to imitations of insects, like scuds, which are small enough to sit on a fingernail.

One evening in a cabin the girls tied their own Pumpkin Head patterns, small green flies with orange beads near the hook eye, that are a general imitation of a mayfly nymph, or a damselfly nymph, or something else. Whatever it is meant to look like, the pattern triggers fish to strike. The next day the girls used those flies to catch several rainbow trout. They were smiling for a long time after that. And it made them more confident at fishing, because they had spun a fly that had fooled a trout. They had gone from casting flies to casting their own spells.

———

I HAVE BOXES OF FLY TYING MATERIAL in my office, collected in the field, given by friends, or bought. Over the years an entire ark of precious animal samples has been found.

I got some of the rarest material—polar bear, wolf, and arctic fox—in a native crafts store in Yellowknife, a small former gold-mining town on the shores of Great Slave Lake, in Canada's Northwest Territories. The seamstress, a Tlicho woman who smelled sweetly of smoked moose hide, made beaded moccasins trimmed with beaver fur and hooded winter parkas with wolf-fur collars. She gave me a paper bag full of scraps for five dollars.

"What you want that for?" she said of the raggedy strips of fur.

"I will tie flies," I said. "And I'll catch pike and lake trout and grayling on them."

She looked at me carefully for a moment, studying my face with an intensity that seemed to look deep into me. "That's good, then," she said finally. "Good to have the fur hunting again."

———

MOST OF THE FEATHERS I HAVE in my fly tying boxes were picked up scattered across the landscape, but some full skins of pheasant and grouse came from friends who hunt. They know I tie and that their castoffs are my treasure. In addition to the polar bear and wolf fur I got in Yellowknife, my fly tying inventory has grown to include yak, musk ox, ostrich, blue heron, black bear, owl, flicker, elk, deer, mountain bluebird, and a wild assortment of barnyard fowl. Some samples are dyed, bringing neon colors and electric flash to the natural tones.

When I lift the lids on the storage boxes the fly tying materials catch the light and invite touching. But it is only in the water, arrayed artfully and tied securely along the shank of a hook, that the material really comes to life. Small twists of hackle feather taken from the cape of a chicken imitate the legs of insects, flexing with the current, or creeping on the surface with the slightest breeze. Marabou, down from a turkey, is so light it undulates underwater like an eel, and a strip of polar bear hair internalizes the light, imitating the translucent back of a minnow. A few strands of Flashabou, a plastic-like material that seems made from shredded lightning, sparkles the way a stream of air bubbles does, entrained in dark water, catching the attention of predatory fish.

Swinging across a salmon river, inching over a weed bed in a lake, bristling on the surface with legs a-twitch, the fly I tied on a hook locked in a vice springs to life. And if I am lucky, a fish seeing it begins to quiver with instinctive urge.

Sometimes the fish's interest fades. Sometimes the fly moves in an odd, unnatural way that warns the fish it lacks life, and lacking life, is not worth eating. Flies that fail quickly fall into disuse in the fly box. They are eventually cast aside or stripped back to the bare hook and returned to the tying vice. But sometimes there is magic and fish are repeatedly drawn to a fly by the light it refracts, or by its shape, or by the natural movement of the fur or feathers.

"When I am tying a fly I never know if it will work or not," I told the girls as we sat at the vice. "I study the texts written by masters in fly tying books and try to copy them, but often I can never quite seem to match their attractive presentation or intricate detail. A well-tied fly is a work of art. Mine, by comparison, often look clumsy. But sometimes the homely flies I tie just work; they are spellbinding."

A small shrimp evolves on my vice. It has legs of trimmed hackle feather; a body of green yarn with a single strand of Flashabou entwined within it; a back made from a strip of plastic; a shell hardened with clear glue. It looks not exactly like a real shrimp, but something that certainly is shrimpish—and it catches fish after fish after fish. After it has taken twenty trout I cut it from my line and put it in a special place in my fly box, afraid to lose it. Later I take it out and put it under a magnifying glass, wondering what makes it so distinct, so irresistible.

"Why does this fly catch more trout than any other shrimp pattern I have ever tied or bought?" I asked my daughters. We had pondered it, turned it over in our hands, passed it back and forth, held it up to see if there was something hidden within the translucent body.

"I can't tell why it's different," said Emma.

And yet there was something unseen that made it magical. There was a spell hidden within. Fly fishers have struggled to divine such secrets for generations. And none have succeeded yet.

———

ONCE I SAT WITH A prawn fisher in his home on the Sunshine Coast. On the living room coffee table was a prawn trap.

"My wife left me," he said. "So, yes, I can bring prawn traps in the house if I want to."

The home, the truck in the driveway, and the commercial prawn boat at the dock had all been paid for by his catches over the years. He knew tides, knew boats, knew prawns, knew traps.

"But this trap," he said, "is a mystery to me."

He set his traps in a long line in the Strait of Georgia. Let them settle two hundred feet, to the bottom. When he came back to pull them up sometimes they were full, sometimes empty, sometimes they had a few handfuls of prawns.

But coming over the transom there was always one trap that held a bounty.

"Same bait in all of them," he said, looking at the trap on his coffee table. "But this trap is always full of prawns. I pull a whole string of traps and get almost nothing in most of them, but this one is full. Always. I can change where I put it on the string. Doesn't matter. This one catches prawns when the others don't, or it catches a hell of a lot more when the other traps only catch some."

He sounded frustrated, even a little angry.

"So what's the problem?" I asked.

He sighed. "The problem is I can't figure out why this trap works. If I could have twenty traps like this, a hundred traps like this, imagine what a season I'd have. I'd have it made."

After every fishing season ended he brought the trap home with him, put it on the coffee table, and slowly surrounded it with empty beer bottles. He sat up at night staring at it. He turned it in his hands the way Emma and I turned the magical shrimp fly, examining it from every angle as if the light might reveal a secret inscription hidden somewhere in the workings.

"Sometimes I think I should take it apart, piece by piece, and study it," said the prawn fisher of his trap. "But then I worry that I might not put it back together exactly right and somehow that would change it."

He was afraid if he looked too hard he'd break the spell.

"Maybe it's a spirit thing," said his deckhand, who sat up with him many nights, helping him drink the beer and talking about the trap. "It's mojo. You don't want to screw with that."

"No, I don't, but I got to know what the secret is," said the prawn boat captain. "Sometimes I leave it at home just to see if the other traps perform better when it's not on the boat. But they don't. Now when I lower it over the side I think, 'What if this is the last time I see it? What if I lose it?' So I got to know, so I can make another one."

I feel that way about the flies I tie. If I catch a great fish I will often cut that fly off and put it aside in my box, to study later, to try and replicate it. It's a futile business.

Once I caught a great steelhead on a Green Butt Skunk that a friend had tied. The fly is supposed to have a tail of red calf hair, a butt end of chartreuse chenille, a body of dark-purple chenille, and a wing of white fiber that looks like polar bear fur. But he had substituted flat, black wool for the body because he didn't have purple chenille, and the wing was so sparse it looked like he had almost run out of that material too. The butt segment was tied too long, covering half the body instead of just being a small, bright tag. It was an ugly fly, but effective—deadly, in fact. So I tied six just like it. And never caught a steelhead on any of them. My copies lacked something unseen. Only his original worked. Then one afternoon, the ugly fly my friend had tied was gone, disappearing in a huge swirl of water just as the fly picked up speed swinging across the tail of a pool.

"That was a very big Chinook," said my friend Nick, who had been watching the fly swim through the pool.

I reeled in the slack line.

"That was my best steelhead fly," I said, looking at the broken leader. "That was the Green Butt Skunk I took that big steelhead on the Thompson with."

"Oh," said Nick. He could have consoled me with a lie. He could have said: "You can always tie another." But Nick ties too and he knew that wasn't true.

"You are screwed now," he said.

Sometimes I think of that prawn fisher going crazy trying to figure things out, and I tell myself not to overthink the voodoo part of fly tying. Some flies work magic. Some don't. The best thing is to just keep casting and enjoy the spells that fall your way.

———

TYING IS A QUIET PURSUIT, and like forest bathing or fly fishing, is often best done alone. But it can be shared, too, and I like to sit with my daughters, showing them how to tie my favorite patterns.

"It is like cooking," I tell them. "You add all the right ingredients in the right order and you get a sweet, fluffy cake. Make a mistake and you get a tasteless lump."

They learned quickly how to lock a thread to a hook shank, how to layer the materials, and how to form solidly tied, nicely shaped bodies. Emma is methodical. She puts each piece in place carefully and isn't happy unless her fly looks as good as the one in the book. Claire is a free spirit. Her flies are whimsical. But there is a mad kind of science to fly tying, and even though many of the best flies don't look like anything in nature, the patterns that make it into the fly tying guidebooks are there for a reason. Books give the step-by-step recipes for tying thousands of trout and salmon flies, and when we reference a text in tying sessions I gently encourage Claire to follow the instructions exactly, because the prescriptions have been developed by experts and some have been handed down through generations. But usually she doesn't listen. Then she goes out on the lake with one of her evolved patterns that has ignored the lessons of the masters—and she catches trout. So there is a creative process performed at the vice that I often don't understand.

AT CHRISTMAS OR ON MY BIRTHDAY there will often be a small package from Claire and inside I will find an assortment of wild fly patterns she has tied. Once there was a small cedar box. On the lid she'd burned a fly fishing scene. Inside was a delightful assortment of bright pink, green, and purple salmon flies. They looked like they should be hung on the earlobes of young women.

"Happy birthday," said the accompanying note. "I feel so lucky that you are my dad. Your endless support and encouragement has made my life and I am so grateful! I have so much fun hanging out with you and Mum. These flies aren't much compared to what I've lost of yours, but it's a slow and steady start to replacing all I've left in weed beds and trophy mouths."

It was signed with a heart.

There is only one fly left in that box now. Over the years the others caught dozens of pink salmon. Some got lost in fish or on underwater snags. Some may have drifted into other fly boxes and I hope they will resurface sometime, on a day when I need something wild and bright to throw a party and entice a salmon to strike. I never lost the note, though. I kept that safe.

———

I TIE ALONE DURING THE winter months when the weather is often too disagreeable to go fishing. Like fly fishing, or painting, tying is a relaxing pursuit because it takes concentration. And it stirs memories. When I tie that shrimp pattern I recall the day on the still lake, casting a long, floating line across a mirrored surface. The fly was gray and green and sparkling, and whenever it twitched a rainbow would come out of the weeds to engulf it. It had a special power and drew fish after fish.

Some flies just work.

My friend Harvey sent me a plea from the Bella Coola Valley once to say he'd lost a blue and purple fly I'd given him that had taken coho, steelhead, rainbow trout, and Dolly Varden.

"Can you tie me another?" he asked.

I made six. A few weeks later he wrote again.

"That pattern catches everything," he said.

I have no idea why. When I look at it in the water I think it is too thin. I set out to tie a big, burly Intruder fly, a pattern that is supposed to have a large profile and which gets its name because it prompts strikes by intruding into the space of salmon. Somehow I ended up with a slithery, slick little fly that moves like a leech—and yet it catches fish in water where there are no leeches.

One afternoon I watched Harvey working one of those flies through a run. I thought the pattern was pathetic. It didn't look like an Intruder, like a chewy baitfish, but like an emaciated, weak minnow.

And yet, it beckoned. It undulated in the water and whenever Harvey took a step downstream or moved his rod, the marabou feathers shuddered, picking up every movement, flickering with light. When he stripped in line the fly looked frightened, darting, vulnerable, and somehow that insistent tremor of life had been spun from my hands around the shaft of an inanimate salmon hook.

"Fish on," said Harvey a few minutes later, his rod bending against the weight of a salmon. In the depths of the pool a silver fish flashed. "Told you it works."

I QUICKLY CAME TO BELIEVE in the effectiveness of fly fishing when I got my first fly rod because luckily a Mickey Finn came into my possession, sent home with my father from his colleague at the *Victoria Daily Times*. Art Mayse, a wonderful writer whose newspaper columns sometimes dealt with his own love of fly fishing, wanted to support my interest in the great sport. So he sent along a few proven patterns and a note encouraging me to start tying my own flies. The note included some of his old fly tying stuff, hackles and other feathers in envelopes, and a small disc of beeswax that looks like a sacramental wafer. It is used to make tying thread sticky before wrapping it on a hook. I have had that disc fifty years and will pass it on to my daughters one day.

The Mickey Finn, Art told my father, is a good pattern to use when searching for sea-run cutthroat. And that's how I used it, until it disappeared one day in the jaw of a big trout. The fly is traditionally tied with dyed red and yellow hair from a deer or cow tail. The shank of the hook is wrapped in silver tinsel, with a small bright-red tag of thread at the tail end. With its shape and flash it mimics a minnow, and although its colors are unnatural, it attracts the cutthroat. It was one of the first flies I fell in love with, and for a time it became my Muir Creek special, though soon I was on to many other effective patterns.

The invention of the Mickey Finn has been attributed to Quebec fly tier Charles Langevin, who came up with it 1800s. It was known originally as the Assassin. In his book *Fly Fishing Warm Water Rivers*, Joseph Cornwall says the red-and-yellow pattern won praise in 1932 from the American John Alden Knight, who invented the Solunar tables. Knight's tables, published widely in newspapers, predict when fishing will be best, based on the influence of the sun and moon. People soon began to organize their fishing trips using the Solunar tables.

Gregory Clark, a popular Canadian journalist at that time who wrote for the *Toronto Star* (and who befriended another young *Star* reporter who loved to fly fish, Ernest Hemingway) noted Knight's endorsement of the Canadian fly. Clark mentioned the pattern in one of his columns, and in the brassy style that helped make him a popular writer, he described the fly as being as dangerous as a Mickey Finn, a spiked drink that knocks out its victims. The new name stuck, and the Assassin's original title was soon forgotten.

Some say the fly existed before Langevin tied it and was simply known as the Red and Yellow Bucktail. Whatever its origins are, there can be no doubt that it works, and it seems to work just about anywhere on any kind of fish.

———

ONE WINTER MY FRIEND HARVEY complained he was seeing lots of sea-run cutthroat in a coastal river he fished, but he was getting only a few on a Muddler Minnow, a big, bushy headed fly that imitates a sculpin and which was one of our favorite patterns. The trout would pluck tentatively at the fly, he said, "but they aren't really interested in it and just hit now and again."

The fish weren't certain if they wanted to bite or not. They were lackadaisical, desultory. I told him to try a Mickey Finn, the pattern I used as a boy to catch sea-run cutthroat. The next day Harvey sent me an image of a four-pound trout with a red-and-yellow fly pinned in its jaw.

"I got this Christmas picture for you," he wrote. "Cutthroat with Mickey Finn fly." A few days later he sent a picture of the same fly, hooked in the mouth of a ten-pound steelhead.

That winter I sat at the vice on a few nights when the girls weren't too busy with their studies, and we tied some flies for a camping trip that was planned for the following summer. We were going to a remote beach on the West Coast of Vancouver Island and I knew we might catch some black sea bass near the kelp beds.

I watched Emma carefully building a Mickey Finn. She was determined about whatever she did and never grew frustrated. Her fingers were nimbler than mine, and she bound the hair to the hook with careful, precise turns.

"Red and yellow calf tail, some silver tinsel," she said listing off the ingredients. "Anything else?"

"Yes," I said. "A lot of hope. Add that in there."

She looked at me quizzically for a moment and shook her head in disapproval. No mythmaking for her.

But Claire leaned over and made a sprinkling motion with her fingers.

"And a little magic," she said.

HESQUIAT

FOR THIRTY YEARS THE four friends, all former wilderness guides at Strathcona Park Lodge, spent at least part of their summers together on a beach on Hesquiat Peninsula. To make room for tents and a cooking fire, they cut openings in dense thickets of salal, an understory shrub prolific in Pacific Northwest rainforests. Salal has raspy green leaves and fuzzy blue berries that attract bears. Raw they are harsh and rough to the human palate, but cooked they soften, adding a pleasant tartness to food.

Maggie's brother Clark, his partner, Bunny, and their old friends Doug and Sue had invited us to join them at their annual summer escape in the wilderness. We picked salal berries with our daughters and added them to pancakes, savoring the sharp sweetness just as coastal Indigenous people had for thousands of years before. The first people usually ate the berries dry, or mixed them with salmon eggs. And they used to dip the berries into the clear, bitter oil rendered from eulachon, a tiny smelt so rich that when dried, then lit with a match, its body burns like a candle.

Eulachon live in the ocean but like salmon return to fresh water to spawn. Historically they returned in such numbers that the water turned black as massive schools moved into the estuaries. Birds gathered like storm clouds above them, gulls and terns diving in wild abandon while sea lions, salmon, and seals slashed into the schools from below. And the people in the villages came running with excitement when they saw that; they knew the feasting was about to begin.

Eulachon return to the rivers in the early spring, usually around Easter, providing Indigenous communities with the first really rich meals of the year, after hungry winters. The early missionaries saw a chance to exploit the link between the resurrection of Jesus, which Easter celebrates, and the end of starvation in lean winters. So they called eulachon the Salvation Fish, or Savior Fish, attributing their return to an act of God. The Nuu-chah-nulth, in whose territory we were camping at Hesquiat, were primarily whaling people, but they would have harvested eulachon if they found them, and certainly they traded with other tribes for eulachon oil, which was a valued commodity long before Captain James Cook sailed into Nootka Sound in 1778, disrupting the Indigenous economy by buying sea otter pelts.

Starting in the early 1990s eulachon populations began to collapse in many British Columbia rivers, including the Bella Coola, Kimsquit, Owikeno, Kingcome, Unuk, and others on the mainland coast. Before the collapse they were plentiful in thirty-three of the province's rivers; the Fraser River alone had a run where the mass of fish was estimated to weigh thousands of tons. Only remnant runs exist in the Fraser and most other mainland rivers now. On Vancouver Island eulachon were known to have been in the Somass River, but it isn't clear what other island watersheds might have had them. None on the island do now.

Eulachon still spawn in some mainland rivers, and a large portion of those fish gather off the West Coast of Vancouver Island, where they concentrate on rich feeding grounds. Unfortunately, the same water that holds eulachon attracts shrimp—and shrimp fishing boats, which drag enormous nets through the area, entraining both shrimp and eulachon. It wasn't until after eulachon populations collapsed in spawning rivers throughout their range that government fisheries biologists realized the commercial shrimp fleet was killing tons of young eulachon in the ocean off Vancouver Island. Special gates and lights were installed on shrimp nets to reduce the unwanted eulachon bycatch, but by the time those methods were implemented, the Savior Fish had almost been wiped out.

Standing on the beach I looked out at the rolling waves knowing that somewhere out there in the depths the last remaining schools of eulachon were gathered in great ephemeral clouds. Then I turned back to see a pillar of smoke rising from our camp, located near the edge of Hesquiat Peninsula Provincial Park. The mountains behind showed great open areas, brown and ragged, where the old-growth forest had been logged. In the park lush forests still stood, a panoply of green, and the contrast between the cut and uncut was shocking.

As I walked the windswept beach, listening to the sea and to the laughter of my daughters, I felt a tumble of emotions. Being in nature brings grace to life and children rejoice in it; they delight in sleeping in tents and rising with the sun, in pushing back the night by sitting around a fire in the dark woods. So there was joy in being there and sharing that with my daughters. But the denuded mountains in the distance were a reminder that we had camped balanced on the edge, between land and sea, where the remnants of two great life-forms, the massive schools of eulachon and the ancient rainforests of the Pacific Northwest, were making a last stand.

I was surrounded by beauty, but at the same time I was acutely aware that much of the natural heritage of the world my daughters' generation was inheriting had already been squandered. The exploitation had started more than four hundred years earlier when trappers, fur traders, and settlers first came to what is now Canada. And still there was no letup. Now we were running out of things—moose, mountain caribou, salmon, eulachon—wilderness itself. Adding to that was the climate crisis; the plundered planet was overheating. That night I fell asleep to the distant call of a lone wolf. It was somewhere back on the mountain and its howl seemed lost and searching. In the darkness it reminded me of how much was at stake.

WE FELL INTO AN EASY RHYTHM at Hesquiat, radiating out from the camp to explore, carrying drinking water from a distant stream, picking salal berries that left our fingers stained, collecting blue mussels from the encrusted rocks, and catching cod in the kelp forests that grew in near shore waters. I cast a Mickey Finn along kelp beds and pulled out black sea bass—the fly I had tied with my daughters while dreaming of just such a moment. To get rock cod, deepwater fish lurking in crevasses on the bottom, the girls used spinning rods and dropped heavy jigs over the side of the boat. They pulled up brightly colored cod and proudly carried them back to camp. Some days we lived entirely off the land and the sea, harvesting all that we needed to eat.

Hesquiat is a Nuu-chah-nulth word meaning "people of the sound made by eating herring eggs off eel grass," according to *British Columbia Place Names*, by G. P. V. and Helen B. Akrigg. We didn't find any herring eggs, which cling like tiny, clear pearls to seaweed, but couldn't have safely eaten them if we had. Harvesting raw herring eggs, long a cultural tradition of Indigenous people, had become a risky business. Because of warming waters in some coastal areas, the eggs posed a cholera risk. "There is evidence suggesting that climate change, including rising temperatures, increases the risk of infections associated with the [*Vibrio cholerae*] bacteria," the provincial Island Health office stated in 2019. So put that down as another loss, another deduction from the world's riches.

————

TO LIVE ON THE EDGE, to camp where the sound of waves is constant, to see the beach brilliant with moonlight, to hear the forest at night, is to feel part of the land and part of the sea. Living like that it was easy to understand how West Coast Indigenous cultures came to believe people transformed from animals or sea creatures. At our camp the separation between the human and natural world slowly dissolved.

Once when Maggie and Clark were out paddling with Emma, the great shadow of a whale passed under their canoe. An oceanic bulk rose to gently break the surface, like darkness breaching. It spewed an aqueous mist that drifted in the air, enveloping the canoe.

"It smelled like rotten cabbage," said Maggie, and Emma grabbed her nose and laughed.

"It stank," she said.

The whale's breath was redolent with fish oil, and I had to wonder if perhaps they had smelled the eulachon even if we never did see them.

Often we would drift with the tide along rough, black reefs, casting to the edge of kelp beds. The constant crash of the waves, the sharp cries of gulls, the startled looks of seals surfacing near us enthralled the girls. They never complained, even though Claire grew pale from seasickness on one outing, and they showed no signs of boredom as we fished for hours, looking for dinner.

We searched for giant lingcod off Hesquiat, hoping to catch one for a village feast. But they had become rare, having largely been "fished out" all along the West Coast by sports and commercial boats. Instead of catching big lings, we caught much smaller rock cod and black bass. We kept just enough for a camp meal and that night, sitting around the fire under a sky as deep as the sea, I told the story of the last great ling I had seen.

As a boy I used to fish in Saanich Inlet for bluebacks, coho that have been in salt water for about one year. Above the lateral line they were the color of the night sky just after sunset, a deep, navy blue, and that's how they got their name. We trolled Mickey Finns and other bucktail flies for them behind a clinker-built boat powered by a knocking Briggs and Stratton engine. My father liked to steer the boat, putting along the shoreline, until a small salmon—usually about two pounds—would rip out of the water to pull down one of our flies. We'd stop the boat to play the fish on light fly rods.

One salmon my father was fighting dove deep beneath the boat and then yanked hard, as if it had suddenly become much stronger. It came up slowly. Resisting with a brute force that didn't seem possible for such a small salmon.

"It feels strange," said my father, bending into the rod. "What the heck have I hooked?"

I leaned over the stern with the net ready, peering into the water. Then, a giant brown head with fierce yellow eyes came rushing up out of the dark water. The face of a massive lingcod materialized just inches away. Its jaws were festooned with teeth and it seemed to be grinning. Then it opened its mouth. A small salmon, its eyes bulging, my father's fly hooked in its jaw, was caught crosswise in the cod's mouth. When the cod snapped its teeth shut it bit the salmon in half. With a quick movement of its massive head, it swallowed both pieces, leaving shards of skin and sparkling scales swirling in the water.

"I will never forget the mouth of that huge lingcod," I said. "I thought it was going to lunge and grab me by the head. But it sank slowly away. The last thing I saw was its yellow eyes glowing, fading away in the blackness."

It was my version of a ghost story, and the girls shuddered. In the silence after, and there is always silence after a good story, a fragment of rock skipped on the Earth's skin. The girls made silent wishes as the meteor streaked over the sea and the sleeping fish within, over the mountains and the fractured forest.

It was Claire's birthday. She was twelve and had grown into a thoughtful, reflective child who practiced her dance routine on the windswept beach, doing graceful pirouettes in the sand. And cartwheels. She was lying on her back now, feet to the campfire, her sister and mother beside her.

"When Emma was born," I said, "Expo '86 was being held in Vancouver, on False Creek near where we lived on Kits Point. There were fireworks every night for weeks, lighting up the sky over our home. It was to celebrate the world fair, but I always said it was for Emma.

"And Claire, four years later—you got the Perseids."

The girls didn't say anything, but both were smiling.

Across the sky above our camp, shooting stars left dazzling streaks as the Earth passed through a debris field trailing behind Swift-Tuttle, a comet wandering the inner solar system. The comet's broken flecks, traveling at 140,000 miles per hour, were burning up in the Earth's atmosphere, illuminating the night sky.

The Perseid meteor shower peaks on the day Maggie gasped, looking up at a white ceiling, and Claire, struggling with the umbilical cord wrapped around her neck, miraculously fell through space and into our life. Emma was sixteen now, and young adulthood was tugging her out of my orbit. As I watched her running on the beach, diving wildly into the cold sea to swim, I wondered how many more trips like this we would share.

———

THE NEXT DAY WE PICKED our way along the shoreline, peering into tidal pools cupped in dark, volcanic rock, waving rich with sea plants. In one the movement of a shadow revealed a sole with a perfectly camouflaged, partially translucent body. Two tiny green eyes, apparently amazed to be caught in such invisibility, stared up, then with a shudder it slipped beneath a cloak of fine sand. Shadow and fish gone forever.

Claire stared into the pool, not quite believing what she had seen.

Nearby the great Pacific, thunderous and heavy, broke against the shore. We stopped to gaze at a thistle seed, caught on a thread of spiderweb. It rose and fell like a dry fly on the end of a fine leader until the anchor line broke and the seed sailed over a rock ledge and across the tide pool, inside which lived the fish that nobody could see. Sometimes the whole wondrous world is held together by a single thread.

Claire and Emma wandered from pool to pool, lifting rocks to watch crabs scuttle away, feeling the rubbery texture of seaweed, collecting small seashells; still as curious about the world, as delighted by its intricacies, as they were when they were little girls.

On a nearby island the trees on the windward side leaned away from the Pacific. The inshore breeze was so steady they had given up trying to stay straight and had grown at an angle to let the wind slide over them. They were shaped by the memory of the wind.

Above the high-water mark left by winter storms, the bleached trunks of drift logs sprawled in a great jumble. They were the whale bones of an ancient forest, dragged out to sea by floodwaters in rivers, stripped of bark and limbs by the tumultuous ocean and then cast back on the shore.

On a log near where we went to draw water from a spring, we found claw marks where a bear clambered up on its daily rounds. It used the long, straight drift log as a sidewalk. At the end of the trunk we could see where the bear jumped down, in repeated trips boring a tunnel through the thick salal. The opening to the trail was marked by tufts of wiry black hair caught on twigs. The bear trail went behind our camp, but our food remained safe because it was stored in sealed buckets hanging from ropes, high in a tree, like a giant mobile in a rainforest.

———

ONE MORNING I ASKED THE GIRLS to go for a hike with me. To look at places we hadn't seen. They agreed and we walked along the coast following a faint path. On a rocky point we stopped to look out at a vast, vacant sea. As we scanned for whales, waves pounded into blowholes bored into the rocks beneath our feet and small spouts of water shot up in front of us. The waves hit so hard the shore shuddered, as if the whales were hiding in the earth, singing and spitting jets of seawater.

The path we were following seemed to have ended nowhere, at a rocky outcrop, but we glimpsed a beach beyond, and we sat on a patch of grass to have lunch and ponder how to proceed. It looked like we could climb down the rock face, run across a narrow strip of sand exposed between waves, and scramble up the rocks on the far side. I was tempted, because all it required was that we understand the timing of the ocean. But as I watched a wave broke out of synch with the others, pushing so deep into the slot it would have hit us had we been trying to cross just then. I imagined a wave dragging us out to sea; unyielding, unforgiving. So that route was not an option. Emma suggested we duck our heads and crawl into the salal like bears. Her uncle Clark had taught her how to tunnel into the shoreline bush in search of Japanese fishing net floats. The beachcombing treasures, baubles of green glass that drifted across the Pacific, could sometimes be found far above the high-water mark, where winter storms tossed them.

Emma's determination and trail-finding skills came in handy. On hands and knees she led the way, with Claire following. They disappeared into the thick brush. After a moment they called back to say they had found a tunnel through the salal; they had found the road to nowhere actually led somewhere, and I started crawling after them. The overgrown trail led us past the dangerous gap in the rocky shoreline and over a headland to a great sweeping beach beyond. We walked through a field of rasping grass and out into the open. And there was a bear, turning over blankets of seaweed at the tide line, rolling it up like a gardener turning sod.

We could get around the bear by walking close to the water's edge, so we shouted, whistled, and clapped our hands as we went, hoping it would move away. But it continued to feed, head down, not hearing because of the wind and not seeing us with its face buried in seaweed and flies.

"Let's stay together and keep walking," I said as we got closer. The girls nodded.

I slipped the bear spray out of my pocket and held it in my right hand, thumb on the release tab, finger on the trigger.

"Keep your arms up. Look big," I said.

We went on and the bear looked up, looked down, looked up again, then started running toward the forest. It glanced back over its shoulder one last time before vanishing into the salal thicket we had just left. Perhaps it was his trail that had led us here.

Back at camp that evening Emma and Claire just shrugged when I recounted the bear story. They told their mother it was nothing to worry about.

The next morning they started gathering pieces to build a mobile, which the women would show them how to make.

They collected the bones of sea creatures, chips of sculpted wood, and rocks holed by the sea. They hunted the beach at low tide and would not rest until the mobiles were completed. Fishing line secured the bones and wood pieces and the feathers of shorebirds in such a fine balance that when the wind blew, all the parts moved, as if telling a story. The mobiles were hung from drift logs near the camp, and in the breeze there was the faint, clinking sound of wood striking bone.

Our friend Sue taught the girls and Maggie how to strip long strands of cedar bark from a tree. They soaked the bark in water to make it soft, and weaved it into mats and baskets. The women sat on the rocks by a tide pool while they worked. Their skin was brown, their hair golden from the sun and the sea wind. They weaved caramel- and chocolate-colored strips of bark together and I watched them, wishing the moment would never end.

I looked up to see shorebirds running along the beach where the waves broke. They plunged their beaks into the saturated sand, straining life. Gulls wheeled over the island and sea otters splashed in the bay as they dove to catch Pacific purple sea urchins. Fur traders wiped out sea otters in the nineteenth century, and that caused urchin populations to explode. Swarms of urchins soon devoured kelp forests all along the West Coast, creating oceanic barrens. Fish and marine bird species collapsed. Then, in the 1970s, otters were reintroduced. They feasted on sea urchins and that allowed the kelp beds to grow back. Slowly black cod, herring, other fish, and birds were starting to return.

All the parts in the diorama spread before us moved, hanging together like a mobile made from the sea, the sky, and the forest. And it had always been this way.

Near camp a black reef emerged at low tide. It was called the Dragon's Back and it reminded us of how old the world was. The reef was encrusted with antediluvian seashells: minarets and twirls of calcium from when the ocean was young. When the tide came in, the reef sank beneath the surface, and the waves above it rippled in the shape of vertebrae, making it seem like the ocean itself was an ancient, living creature.

———

SMALL GROUPS OF HIKERS WENT PAST our camp sometimes and they usually stopped to talk, surprised to find such a permanent settlement in the salal in the middle of nowhere. We told them where to find drinking water on the beach trail ahead, where the bears liked to feed, and how to get past the headland where the trail fell into a tidal crevasse.

"Shout first to make sure a bear is not on the trail," I said. "Then take the path to nowhere."

Sometimes friends came in to visit us at the camp, staying for a few days. One visitor, who came with his wife and adult daughter, became the campfire tender, collecting ancient driftwood and rendering it to charcoal to make a cooking oven. He spent all day nurturing it while the others went hiking and said his great ambition was to create a perfect fire. His passion glowed in his joyous soul. He told a story he heard about a tandoor oven in India that had been burning continuously for a hundred years.

"Generations of fire tenders keep it burning," he said, lost in the rapture ancient fire makers knew.

"Did you know that eulachon burn?" I asked. "Imagine taking a fish from the water and burning it like a candle. They spit and sparkle like the meteors we saw in the sky last night."

We agreed if we ever found a dead eulachon on the beach we would dry it and make a candle, a token, a burning memorial to the lost Fish of Salvation.

At night the fire drew out stories. Looking into the flames, the woman married to the fire tender told us that twenty-five years earlier, after being away six months in Nicaragua, he came home to tell her he had left a wife and a child there.

She looked into the fire and said she took him back; to raise with him the children they had in Canada, to choose one pain over another. Her husband sat at the perfect fire he had been burning for days, listening silently as the wood he had collected snapped and the years vanished in smoke. We were not sure why this story had been shared. But it seemed like a tribal rite, a story that needed to be said around a campfire. The truth sometimes flickers like a flame; it burns and goes up into the dark sky.

The campfire tender was still. Light danced around him and he stared endlessly into the flames.

That night a storm shook our tents in the sea of salal. Whale Bone Bay, which lay nearby, was rearranged whenever a big wind coincided with a high tide. The sands shifted under an irresistible ocean surge and part of the whale that settled in the shallows decades ago, bearing the wisdom of the depths, surfaced again. Or so the legend said.

Doug knew this. He had known this from years of camping at Hesquiat. It wasn't known whether the whale came into the bay to die, or if its carcass had drifted in after its death. But either way, once there, it lay as still as the ocean would allow, gently rocking after its last vaporous breath was spent, until it sank gently into its grave. For a century sand fell on it like pollen.

There were stories told that following a big wind, bones emerged and got washed up onto the beach. The whale kept coming in a piece at a time in Whale Bone Bay, and nobody knew what might be next. Maybe a bone embedded with a Nuu-chah-nulth spear point?

Anything cast on a beach by one wave can be taken back by another, or by the next high tide. Knowing this, Doug went searching, beachcombing just after dawn, to find the night's high blow had freed a single rib. He carried it back and laid it on a drift log near the fire ring, offering a holy relic to camp, proof the legend of the whale was true. Everyone marveled at the beauty and surprising lightness of the rib; it seemed like something that came from a giant bird and it was wondrous to hold.

One day a small plane with oversized tires dropped down from the clouds and bounced along the sand beach that had emerged at low tide. Len, a friend, had dropped in for a visit. He brought ice cream. Before it melted, before the tide came in, he had to take off, fretting over a propeller that had been slightly damaged in the landing. We saw him soar off over the forest, over the mountain, but that night, just before dusk, an inflatable boat came in to the beach at high speed. Two Canadian Coast Guard officers clambered ashore. Len's flight plan hadn't been closed. He hadn't landed and hadn't radioed in a change of routes, so a search was underway. We pointed to where we'd last seen him in the sky, a small, dark shadow going east. That night we watched a ship searching the bay, listening in the black, silent sea for a signal sent by the aircraft's emergency locator beacon, and we sat at the fire, feeling sick and hopeless. All they heard were the call of whales. The next day the camp radio crackled with a call from the Coast Guard; the plane was found, torn apart in the forest; the pilot miraculously safe. Life hangs by a thread, always.

———

ONE QUIET MORNING WE HIKED the Elder's Trail, which snaked across a point covered by primordial forest, a small wedge of land that had been saved from logging. It reminded us of how the world once was: tall and green and breathtaking in its splendor.

The trail twisted through roots, groves of ferns, and moss as it took us away from the bright beach away from the sun and into the shady, cool forest. To go there was to enter another dimension. In the forest the sound of surf faded away, until all we heard were branches moving softly in the wind. The light became dense and soft, glowing green like chlorophyll.

Emma and Claire, waist-deep in ferns, left the path to lean against a massive cedar tree. Its trunk was so large that when five of us tried to link our arms around it, we could not close the gap. We reached, like roots searching in the earth, to find each other's fingertips. It felt like we were trying to embrace a beached whale. Small warblers, visible only when they moved, rang like chimes in the canopy far above.

The trail demanded every step be perfect. Rocks as slick as skinned bones hid in the moss; there were trip holes, stumble places, and roots set like snares. Giant old trees leaned over the trail in cathedral columns and we walked carefully among them, silent as monks. The trail tightened, grew darker, narrower, and then, as suddenly as we'd entered, we emerged from the forest. The abrupt transition from dark back to light was dazzling. The aperture clicked open and we were left blinking on the edge of a white beach. We were glistening with forest dew and spiderwebs, amazed to see a beach curving away from us like an exotic travel poster. In the distance a river ran into the sea. Emma and Claire carved a heart in the sand and then ran ahead, gamboling like otters while the adults walked along behind.

We went to the river and swam in water so cold it felt like we had plunged into fire. I jumped in the water and jumped out almost as quickly. Sue swam out and sat on a rock in the middle of the river, warming her naked body in the sun. When she plunged back in she whooped from the cold shock, from the joy. Emma and Claire dove under and came up spouting like whales, like blustery sea lions. After a week of bathing in the ocean, it felt good to wash the salt off our bodies. We were made pure by water that had run off a snowfield on a distant mountain.

THAT NIGHT AROUND THE CAMPFIRE, Doug, a big bear of a man who liked to thump out folk songs on his guitar when he was not collecting whale bones, told the story of how as a wilderness guide he used to take teenagers into the forest and leave them there alone, so they could mark their passage to adulthood by spending a night in isolation.

With a lift of his eyebrows he made a challenge. And Emma said she was ready. The next day she, Doug, and Clark repaired a sweat lodge on a nearby point that became an island when the tide came in. It would serve as a shelter for Emma's night of passage. After dark, at low tide, she took her sleeping bag and walked down the beach alone with a flashlight. I watched the light bobbing into the distance, past where I had crossed fresh wolf and bear tracks in the past few days, and where we once saw the paw prints of a mountain lion, round, padded, and wicked.

I knew that not far from our camp a man had saved his wife from a cougar attack by driving a spear into the animal as it wrestled with her in their forest garden. She told me the story of her scars and the sound the lion made biting her head. And at the end she said: "I forgive the lion."

I breathed deeply as Emma vanished into the darkness, and tried to stay calm, but later I lay awake listening to the forest of the night. Near midnight I dressed, made my way down the beach, and sat on a drift log a hundred yards from the sweat lodge. I couldn't get closer because the tide had come in, filling the channel. She was alone out there, on a small island, the black sea running between us, a vast scattering of stars above.

I went back to my tent shivering. Maggie was lying awake waiting for me. We talked quietly, each trying to soften the other's fear, to temper our parental angst.

"She's growing up so fast," said Maggie, and I sensed in her the same pride, the same fear of separation, the same loss that I felt. We lay together holding hands. I got up again in the night, sometime before dawn, went out looking in the flashlight beam for the gleaming eyes of bears or wolves. There was nothing but darkness. I saw the tide was slowly dropping, slipping back out to sea carrying bits of driftwood, but it still had a long way to fall. On my way back I looked into the girls' tent, pitched next to ours, and saw Claire sleeping blissfully. I had forgotten she was alone that night too. She was close enough we could hear her if she called out, but I was reminded she was growing too and one day would follow Emma.

I WAS UP EARLY THE NEXT MORNING, building a fire, sending smoke out over the water in a soft, blue tendril that seemed to be searching for something as it made its way toward Whale Bone Bay and the Dragon's Back. I could see new wolf tracks in the sand between our camp and the sweat lodge. That night two animals had loped between us, stopping to scent the air before going on toward the Elder's Trail.

Later that morning Emma came down the beach, her sleeping bag draped over one shoulder. She sat at the fire smiling.

"I thought if I got scared that I could always come back to camp," she said. "Then the tide came in and I was trapped. The water came right up to the sweat lodge door and I knew I'd have to stay the night. So I just went to sleep."

She spoke with quiet confidence and I realized the child we raised had become a young woman, and the wild land was in her. It always would be now.

I was proud of her, but unbalanced too by the sense of separation I felt, by the disconnection, by the untethering of planets, the loss of gravity.

I hadn't sought fatherhood, but it found me, and the children had bound me to life in ways I had never imagined. Now my first child was grown, and was drifting away. She had to go, I knew that, because the river never stops flowing to the sea. But it is not easy.

———

A FEW DAYS LATER THE VILLAGE at Hesquiat was dismantled bit by bit, piece by piece, like whale bones uncoupling from a resting place. The camp went into stuff sacks and plastic bins tied tight with scraps of rope. On the last night we took down the big tarp that had shielded the kitchen from rain, and nighthawks swooped into the clearing in the salal, passing so low we heard the air in their feathers as they turned to catch bugs and to snatch campfire ash rising like insects in the smoke.

The next morning we waited for the incoming tide to lift Clark's boat from the sand where it had rested. The sea crept over the beach, turned the point with the sweat lodge into an island again, and washed away the tracks left by the wolves.

"I want to stay all summer," said Claire as we pulled away from Hesquiat, the boat loaded with a jumble of camp gear. There was a serenity about her that you wouldn't expect in a twelve-year-old; she had grace. Around one wrist she wore a bracelet, made from twisted strands of cedar bark that had been softened in a tide pool, weaving together the sea and the forest.

Looking back as we pulled away from the beach, Emma said she was surprised to see how close the sweat lodge was to where our tents had been in the openings cut in the salal.

"That night I felt so far away," she said laughing. "And you guys were actually right there all the time."

Yes, we were, but the dark tide intervened and wolves walked between us, their danger and beauty hidden in the night. That's the way the world works. A lot of things just aren't seen. The trick is to learn not to be afraid of the unknown, I suppose.

I sat with my arm around Emma's shoulder, looking out to sea for whales. The boat pitched in the waves and as it lurched I felt the line drawing tight between us, tugging.

When the thread breaks the thistle blows away with the wind. I knew that, but knew too that a sense of nature was embedded in her and Claire now, and that was something we would always share.

III
ALLUVIUM

"In the depth of our being we have a longing to
know the Earth and its plan, to know the universe
and ourselves in its deepest and truest form,
and to know Ultimate Reality."

FATHER CHARLES BRANDT

THE
HERMITAGE

SILENCE IS THE ESSENCE OF FISHING. Finding it is as important as finding the fish themselves, and in the rainforests of the Pacific Northwest, under the towering Gothic arches of nature, it is as profound as anything experienced in a cathedral.

One fall day, a few years before the devastating fire of April 2019, I sat in the pews at Notre-Dame de Paris, looking up at the vaulted columns that faded into shadows far above. Nearby Maggie lit a candle in memory of her mother, Nora, a gentle, intelligent woman who died of Alzheimer's disease and whose lush garden our children loved to play in, picking flowers that bloomed like sea anemones. Soft light flowed into the nave through ancient stained glass windows behind the high altar. The cathedral, which is more than 850 years old, is as sacred a place as you can find on Earth, but the sound of tourists shuffling past the alcoves, whispering and taking photos, made me miss the meditative quiet, the oceanic tranquility, of the ancient rainforests I knew.

In the forest, silence is deep, embracing, intoxicating, and the face of creation is close at hand, revealing itself in the touch of fingertips to rough bark, in the sound of a river running through time, in the eyes of an owl, or in the sudden bright color on the skin of a toxic newt, a flash as startling as the amaranth-red sash on a bishop's black cassock.

Father Charles A. E. Brandt, a former Trappist monk who studied ornithology at Cornell University, was drawn to the old-growth forests on Vancouver Island and, in 1966, he became the first hermit priest ordained by the Roman Catholic Church in two centuries. He settled in a small cabin on the banks of Oyster River. For more than fifty years he lived there alone, in communion with nature, meditating, fly fishing, re-binding ancient books as a source of income, bird-watching, and taking photographs. He died on a Sunday morning in October, during the great pandemic of 2020, and I was unable to attend his funeral. He was ninety-seven. We last corresponded just a few months before he died, when I sought permission to quote him in this book, and he seemed as vital as ever. In a memorial posting at the funeral home I described his death as a great loss to the planet.

"Those of us who were lucky enough to know him, however briefly, were blessed indeed," I wrote. "The waters flow on, but the river is diminished."

———

FATHER BRANDT BELIEVED CONTEMPLATING NATURE is being in touch with God, and he dedicated himself to that pursuit. I met him at the hermitage late one day, stopping in as I returned from a trip casting flies for salmon off an ocean beach he had told me of. He was restoring a bible that was centuries old, and above his work table was a photograph of a young, beautiful woman, an activist, who had been arrested a few years earlier for blockading a logging road while trying to save an old-growth forest on Vancouver Island.

"My hero," said Father Brandt, an environmental campaigner who fought to raise public awareness, to save the Tsolum River from pollution and the Oyster River estuary from development.

We shared a reverence for fishing and nature, and we sat together in the forest outside his hermitage, talking for hours. Gentle, soft voiced, kindly, he spoke with a quiet wisdom about life, about the importance of quietness, and about fly fishing.

Surrounded by great trees, we watched darkness expand and the stars emerge, sharp and bright. I told him something I hadn't spoken of before, that I was troubled with thoughts of my own mortality, a heavy feeling that began visiting me shortly after Emma was born and which grew when Claire arrived. As a young man I never thought about death (or deeply about much, to be honest). But when I had children I became acutely aware of my frailties, of the slippage of time, of its onrush, and of the responsibility of what had become the most important role in my life: fatherhood.

Time runs out for all of us, of course, but it wasn't until I had children that I realized how rapidly it vanishes. I was amazed by how quickly they had grown from babies into young girls and were off to school. And I was troubled too by how suddenly a few friends of mine had died. One was an artist who carved birds, trout, and salmon from cedar, and the other wrote books about the rivers of his past. Both were skilled fly fishers who loved the waters I loved. They should have lived much longer but suddenly, their hearts gave out and they were gone. I began to think about death as a stalking presence, a shadowy entity, like the relentless ravens trailing the owl in the forest.

And who would throw stones to protect me?

The awareness of my own pending death wasn't frightening, but it was unsettling, disturbing, like having a silent, unwanted stranger sitting in your living room, refusing to leave. So I talked to Father Brandt about it, hoping he might help.

"I don't want to leave my daughters alone, to vanish on them," I said. "The thought of abandoning them like that desolates me."

Father Brandt looked silently into the forest. After a moment he smiled gently and said not to worry so much. Eventually I would have to leave their physical presence, he said, but becoming nothing, vanishing completely, simply wasn't possible. Death is transforming, he said, but we are made of the same stuff as the stars, as the universe, as the forest around us, and so none of us can just go away.

"You will always be here, somewhere," he said. "Leaving isn't really an option."

Dust to dust, carbon to carbon is what he seemed to be saying.

His view of life took in the whole universe, and he recognized that each of us was just a speck within it, a grain of sand spinning within the current of a great river. Above us the Milky Way swung across the heavens, a spray of light in the vastness, and below us we could hear the Oyster River, running softly through the woods. His answer wasn't an answer, really; it wasn't a direction on how to deal with my bleakness, but somehow I felt at peace, perhaps just because

I'd shared for the first time something that was troubling me. Such is the balm of confession to a priest.

———

FOR MANY YEARS BEFORE HE DIED Father Brandt twice a month hosted meditative retreats at his hermitage, where he discussed inner peace and led contemplative walks through the woods.

At those small gatherings he encouraged people to walk slowly, so they could absorb nature. He called it "walking purposefully." Long after I first talked with him about it, I heard about forest bathing, a practice that gained popularity in North America in the 2000s, but which developed in the early 1980s in Japan, where it is known as shinrin-yoku.

Father Brandt was into forest bathing long before the '80s, however. More accurately, he was into what I will call bathing in nature, because he walked purposefully not just in forests, but in rivers and on ocean beaches too. He waded with his fly rod in the Oyster, Tsable, Tsolum, Campbell, and other waters on Vancouver Island in the same meditative way he walked through the woods.

When I visited Father Brandt he was suffering from an attack of peripheral neuropathy, which made his hands and feet numb. But he was still going for long, contemplative walks on trails and on an old, abandoned logging road in the woods near his cabin.

"I do not think of the road as leading anywhere. It is the road to nowhere, the path on which I have been journeying for a lifetime," he writes in *Self and Environment*. "And although this is a path of nowhere, in reality it is the path to everywhere."

In a lifetime of praying, meditating, and fly fishing, Father Brandt came to understand the sacred power of nature by walking the path to nowhere in the rainforests of the Pacific Northwest.

One of the key beliefs he developed was that people have to stop being so disruptive of creation—that we have to learn how to have a benign presence within it.

"We have to fall in love with the natural world," he said. "We only save something if we love it, and we only love it if we think it is sacred."

One winter, just before Christmas, I wrote about Father Brandt for *The Globe and Mail.* In a weekly environmental column I was then doing for Canada's national newspaper, I described how instead of giving sermons, he emailed his followers photos taken on his spiritual walks in the forest. The face of God is in nature, he had decided, and nothing he could say would improve on that. So his photos arrived without the seasonal religious observations you'd expect from a priest, and with almost no descriptions.

"Last leaf, hermitage," said a typical message. It came with a photo of a single leaf on an otherwise bare tree. That tree, its singular, radiant beauty in a forest, made him bring his slow walk to a full stop.

"Hermit priest Rev. Charles Brandt doesn't send out typical Christmas blessings from his small hermitage," I wrote. "A picture will do.

"Throughout the year, the liturgical seasons pass without Father Brandt reminding his followers of the sacredness of the dates. Instead of delivering prayers by rote, to those on his e-mail list he sends photographs of nature."

One of the pictures he sent me that year was a close-up of a mountain lion gazing into the lens of his camera. It was simply labeled: "cougar."

I asked about the cougar and he told me he was walking near the Oyster River one day when he felt a presence. He didn't see anything, but the powerful sense he wasn't alone stayed with him as he went through the woods to his cabin. He went slowly up the steps onto the porch and when he turned to slide the glass doors shut behind him, he saw it wasn't just God walking with him in the forest that day. A mountain lion was crouched at the bottom of the stairs, its eyes fixed on him, its tail twitching with temptation. The animal and its hunger, or its curiosity, its instinctive need to stalk, had trailed him through the woods. Father Brandt took a photograph, slid the door shut, and made a cup of tea. When he looked again the cougar was gone, but there was a depression in the grass and when he placed his hand there he felt the lingering heat shadow.

We sat near where the mountain lion had lain and talked about fly fishing. Speaking with reverence he told me about going out alone early on New Year's Day and catching a big steelhead "so perfectly formed it seemed a miracle." His voice was full of wonder as he described the rapturous quiet on the solitary river. The whole world seemed still and the great fish, he said, holding his hands apart to show its length, had a belly as white as the snow that fell that day, cloaking the world in silence.

Before age and peripheral neuropathy limited his movement, Father Brandt often went wading in the rivers of Vancouver Island, where among the fly fishing community he was regarded as a sort of water spirit, a blessing you were lucky to encounter.

A friend told me he was steelhead fishing one fall when he saw a dark figure standing on a gravel bar obscured by river mist. "I thought for the longest time it was a black bear," he said. "Then it transformed." The figure became Father Brandt. He came out of the fog carrying a fly rod, wading with purpose, each step counting, each step finding its proper place among the river stones. Father Brandt fished as he walked, slowly, gently, and he often fished by himself. But he never felt lonely fishing, he said, because he bonded "with the other fishers of the river—the mergansers, goldeneyes, herons and kingfishers—as well as the trees along the bank."

He described nature as a sacred society, "not a collection of objects, but a community of subjects to be communed with, not primarily to be used or exploited."

A community of subjects—among which he was just one.

Before I left he gave me a copy of *Self and Environment*, inscribed, "For Mark, and friendship." He also gave me a book of quotations he compiled, *Meditations From the Wilderness*. It is a collection of his favorite nature writing by Aldo Leopold, Henry David Thoreau, Barbara Kingsolver, Annie Dillard, and others. I give copies of that book to friends who need solace, sometimes to friends who are dying. I gave it to my daughters to read. It is full of wisdom.

Father Brandt said that one of the ways he found calmness was by meditating twice a day, and he urged me to try it.

"To meditate one enters into silence, stillness and concentration," he said. "To enter into this silence one takes a holy word, such as God, love, Mary, a little word, and repeats this word—we call this word a mantra—continuously and joyfully... this will eventually lead you into your deep true self and into ultimate reality."

The daily meditation sessions seemed a bit too structured for me. But I realized after talking with Father Brandt that through fly fishing I was on the same journey he was as a hermit priest. I had come, in my own manner, to embrace his philosophy of purposeful walking, to experience fly fishing as something that is transcendental, that leads you into silence and toward meaning.

I had come to understand that the sacredness of nature is more important on a fishing trip than catching fish. And leaving the hermitage that night I realized that to find greater inner peace—to find the deep true self—I would need to fly fish with more awareness and concentration. I could meditate in my own way, and my mantra would be the sound of the cast line, the rhythm of it, moving through the air, over the water and over the forest.

After leaving Father Brandt in the forest I felt my fears of mortality subsiding, ebbing out—not completely vanishing, but softening. I wanted to live long enough to see my daughters grow and have families of their own. I wanted to live long enough to teach them all I knew about fly fishing and life and the importance of nature. But he was right: the river in the forest, the salmon in the trees, and the stars above were all made of the same elements. After death I would still be there somewhere. As he is now.

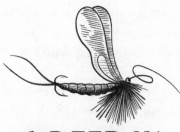

A DEER IN
THE WOODS

IT SNOWED OVER CHRISTMAS and the ferry to Salt Spring Island was nearly empty on Boxing Day morning. My truck cut through two inches of snow, making the first tire tracks up the hill from Fulford Harbour, past St. Paul's, a small stone church built in 1885 by early farming families. In devotion they delivered the granite blocks by canoe, dragged them to the site with oxen, and placed them by hand.

The solid, graceful Catholic church and its graveyard lay silent in falling snow as I drove by on the way to see my mother. She lived in the village of Ganges, working at a seniors' care home on Salt Spring, an island which sits saintly and green, surrounded by the blue waters of the Strait of Georgia.

Pictures of my mother in England during the war show a beautiful young woman with cascading black hair and milky skin, glowing with optimism despite the chaos of the world around her. In 1944 she was one of eighty thousand women in the Land Army, replacing on farms men who went to serve in the military. Like so many other women in her generation, she was pushed out of the workplace when peace returned, and after the war she dedicated her life to motherhood. But her children grew and drifted away, one by one, then her marriage failed, and suddenly she was adrift in the world, alone.

My mother had always seemed a meek and gentle soul, but there was surprising strength hidden in her. And so there she was, late in life, after being out of the workforce for more than twenty-five years, supporting herself with a job in a residential facility where some of the people under care weren't much older than her.

She lived in a small house a few blocks from where she worked, caring for people as they shuffled toward death. The long-term care facility looked out on lawns and flower beds, but it always smelled faintly of bleach and hand sanitizer. Outside the bedrooms, families posted pictures of beautiful young men and women, diving into pools, skating, dressed for parties, or proudly holding awards. Images of lives past. Inside those rooms were the shells of what was left from those times: frail, old people, with broken bodies or failing minds. Some were still mentally bright and articulate, but many were confused and incoherent, wandering randomly through memories. It was the kind of place that reminded me life passes quickly and doesn't end well, no matter how beautiful you are in youth.

Among those in my mother's care was Mima, a sparkling, cheerful ninety-nine-year-old woman who said a man "dressed in brown, with chickadees perching all over him" often visited her to talk of world affairs.

"You just missed my visitor," she said one morning when Mother brought Mima her breakfast tray.

"Which way did he leave?" Mother asked, wondering why she hadn't passed anyone in the hallway.

"He went right through there, into the garden, same way he came in," said Mima, nodding toward a wall.

"She was bright as a button," my mother said, as if to suggest Mima's visitor must have been real enough.

———

I ALWAYS FELT A SENSE OF CALM visiting Salt Spring, where llama farms, quirky art galleries, silent dharma centers, and apparitions covered with birds all had a place. I already knew the island well by the time my mother moved there after her divorce, because during my college days I went fishing there. Its small lakes held rainbow trout, which I caught in the winter, and bass, which I caught in the summer.

The island pace is restrained, contemplative, but that Boxing Day an even deeper quiet fell over everything. The sky was a whirl of snow and the fields lining the road were covered with a blanket as soft as sheep's wool. Smoke rose from houses hidden in the woods, but nothing stirred.

And then I turned a corner and saw a car upside down in the middle of the road. It was a bright-red subcompact, its emergency blinkers flashing. I braked and the wrapped Christmas presents beside me tumbled off the passenger seat onto the floor. My wipers beat steadily, sweeping back the snowflakes. I put on my own four-way flashers, checked the rearview mirror, and stepped out.

The upturned car was vacant. There were no footprints, so fresh snow must have fallen after the accident, but it was as if the driver had simply vaporized, like the ghost that visited Mima. Patches of snow turned orange as the lights blinked on and off. I looked in the ditch for a body, jotted down the license plate number, then drove around the car and several minutes later pulled in to the RCMP station. The clerk calmly wrote down the information, saying a driver had called to report losing control on the Fulford-Ganges Road that night. She looked up with apparent irritation when I said the car was upside down, on its roof on the center line. "It's an accident waiting to re-happen," I said. She said it would be taken care of.

I carried on to deliver the presents to my mom. We had tea and Christmas cake and I heard stories from her about the care home and her long, daily walks in the woods. Often working twelve-hour shifts, my mother relaxed by going on rambles, immersing herself in the pastoral landscape that her patients could only gaze out at. Sometimes she took them out into the gardens, but they weren't able to cross the fields and go into the forest, as she did. "It is terrible to be so old and feeble you can't get out in nature," she said. "I hope that day never comes for me."

———

IT IS ONLY ABOUT EIGHT MILES from the ferry terminal at Fulford Harbour to Ganges, but the road winds through woods and rises over a steep ridge along the way, making it a challenging three-hour hike. Few people make that long walk, but my mother did once, at night, alone. She recounted the story that day after I told her of finding the car lying in the middle of the road. It was as if the image of the car, abandoned in the darkness by its driver, stirred the memory.

She said she got off the last ferry to the island one evening and went for a coffee with a man she knew who lived near the terminal. She didn't say his name and until then had never hinted that she was seeing anyone, despite having been divorced for many years.

"When I left his place it was dark and the last shuttle bus had gone," she said, which meant it must have been around midnight. "He wouldn't give me a ride, so I walked."

It was quiet. There was no traffic; just the sound of her footsteps. She looked up at the stars and about halfway to Ganges, grew tired of walking.

"I went to sleep in the woods," she said, the way some mothers would say they went to their room for a nap. It was fall then, not yet winter, and not so cold, she said. "I lay in the ferns and grass and slept until just before the sun came up."

She said the birds woke her. The dawn chorus, calling in sweet, high notes like the voices of children. And then she saw a deer.

"It walked out of the woods and came so close I could touch it," she said. "I just lay still and it sniffed at me and looked at me, then walked away." She was amazed by the moment; a wild deer so close she could feel its breath on her skin.

"They say there are no deer on Salt Spring, but I know there are because I came face to face with one," she said.

It was a troubling and curious story. There are deer on Salt Spring, so many that farmers and gardeners complain about them at times. The bears and wolves had been eradicated and there are only a few cougars, occasional visitors, but there are lots of deer. Why my mother, whose nature diary had frequent entries about seeing deer, would say people believed there weren't any is a mystery.

There were other questions the story raised. Who was the unknown man? Why had she spent so long with him that she missed the bus, knowing it was the last one? And why wouldn't he give her a ride home in the middle of the night? This did not seem like the caring relationship you would want any woman to be in, especially your mother.

"Just a friend," she said when I gently pressed for more information. Then she got up and put the tea things away; a signal that that conversation had ended.

Driving back to the ferry I slowed on the curve where the car had rested upside down. It had vanished like the driver, like Mima's visitor, birds fluttering on his coat as he passed through the walls.

SOMETIMES WHEN I WAKE NOW to the dawn chorus, to the tumult of bird songs, I think of my mother lying in the forest, the light slowly spreading over her and the silhouettes of the trees moving gently in the wind above. She lies still and looks up in wonder. It is like death, I imagine, with the ethereal light, the choir of birds, and the soft flutter of wings.

The best time to hear birds sing in the city is in the morning, before the sound of rush-hour traffic blots it out. They sing all day, off and on, but in this sweet period the songs rise in such profusion and with such a simple clarity that they seem, for a brief waking moment at least, to be the only thing that exists. One can lie there and wonder if this was the first sound the first people heard in the darkness before revelation, in the Garden of Eden or in the clamshell on the beach.

"They speak the story of the universe," Father Brandt writes of the dawn chorus in *Self and Environment.* And he describes the song of a robin as a canticle, which is a form of hymn. In *Pilgrim at Tinker Creek*, the brilliant nature writer

Annie Dillard describes birdsong as being "just like the garbled speech of infants."

Whether we hear the incoherent babbling of babies or the mnemonic chanting of hymns, we search within birdsong for meanings that may or may not be there. Sometimes we find the truth. It is understandable that people take solace from singing birds, but the dawn chorus is not always what it seems. The songs can be sweet murmurings of joy, but also territorial declarations, warnings against trespass, cries of danger, and expressions of sexual urgings as the chorus rises, then falls silent.

My mother said when the birds woke her in the forest she arose refreshed. She walked home, coming into Ganges as people were stirring, lights going on in their kitchens, their dreams evaporating. She said she was happy because, walking past those homes, she knew something about the sacred day that none of them did. She had been lifted by the dawn chorus and had been touched by the soft breath of a wild deer.

She often felt this way, joyous in knowing nature's intricacies, its secrets. She liked to get up early and go for long rambles through the woods, returning to jot in her field journal observations about birds, deer, rabbits, toads, and a mountain lion, "a brown form that slid over a deadfall."

She often saw things that others didn't.

Once, cutting through the bush following a faint deer trail, she stopped to tie a trail marker to a branch so she could find her way back, and her hand touched a hummingbird's nest. Inside were two tiny, naked chicks, heads bobbling.

"I will of course take care in the future where I leave trail markers," she wrote.

She kept field journals for years, carefully jotting in them after each outing. I found the small, battered notebooks after she died. And in reading them I felt regret about not having known more about her, about not having shared any of those nature walks with her as an adult.

"Have decided to make a few notes—just to look back once in awhile to see how I enjoyed my walks," she writes on the opening page of one diary. "If I can walk I'm happy."

———

MY FIRST HOME WAS IN VICTORIA, where I was born, but it wasn't until I read the journals that I realized we had lived there in "a tiny wood cottage" not far from Swan Lake.

In her notes she writes of a "desperate winter" in that small house, with two boys under four, Stephen and Timothy, and me a newborn. That December there was a heavy snowfall. "It had been a pickers cabin, on a daffodil bulb acreage. It was almost buried," she wrote. "It was soft snow. But I was tired from caring for two small children and nursing the baby. The little boys watched from the window as I toiled away. When I did reach the wood stack it was frozen solid and had to be hacked free . . . Dear heaven, it was hard to get the wood to the kitchen and start a fire with wet kindling to make breakfast porridge. Hard times. If I do have a place in Canada, it didn't come easy."

My mother had always wanted to have a daughter, but instead gave birth to five boys. And she miscarried early once. "That was my baby girl," she used to say. When I had two daughters she drew them to her with boundless love. Often she would call and say: "I'm on the ferry from Salt Spring. Coming to see the girls," and later would arrive at our doorstep in Vancouver with dolls or other presents she'd made. She'd disappear upstairs or into the garden with the girls, not interested in adult company, content to spend all day with the children, reading books, doing art projects, telling stories about faeries, or going for walks around nearby Trout Lake Park. It was touching that such gentleness remained in a woman who had lived through a war and whose dream of growing old in her own family home had been shattered.

She said people flooded out of England after the war because peace didn't bring relief to an exhausted country. Food rationing became more severe after the war when US aid shipments ended, and jobs for women disappeared when the soldiers came home from the front. She was decommissioned from the Land Army; others were turned out of factories and offices, even though they had mastered their trades and kept the economy running.

Even for men work was hard to find. And for my father there was the added challenge of not having a war record to boast of on his résumé. No medals, no commendations, no combat stories, just time served as a conscientious objector.

In Victoria he got a new start. He worked delivering milk, and then on a garbage scow before getting the job he dreamed of, working as a reporter on a small newspaper. After that we moved often as he pursued his journalism career. Always another newsroom, another house, another town, and my mother holding the family together as best she could on a small allowance for food and clothing. I remember walking to the grocery store with her and all she had was twenty dollars to feed the whole family for a week. Somehow she filled the cart, with both of us checking the price on each item and keeping a running total. At the checkout we nervously waited to see if our math was right, fearing the embarrassment of having to put items back on the shelf because there wasn't enough money.

But despite such hardships, most of the entries in my mother's journal aren't laments about a difficult life, or expressions of bitterness about broken dreams, but rather are the observations of a naturalist, at peace in the field.

"Blustery dull day. Wild tossing of small birds as they attempt to fly," reads one. "No deer today—spring is getting ready to burst. Sparrows in the hedge. Pick, pick, pick."

In another she writes: "I can always tell when there is a disturbance drifting toward the coast. The birds seem alarmed and the sea gulls take over the soccer field."

And this, written like an extended haiku:

> *On the roadside*
> *A plump black beautiful rabbit*
> *In the hedgerow*
> *Chickadees and finches*
> *On the golf course—deer—*
> *In the ditch—garbage*
> *And garbage is*
> *Signs of a spoiled*
> *People.*

She walked or rode her bike every day. If she saw a game trail leading off into the bush, she would follow, to see where it went. Most days her field entries were short and rarely contained deep, inner thoughts, but there is beauty in simple observation.

"Woven in last season's robin's nest—strips of plastic and horsehair," was typical. Or: "The leafless trees look lacy against the sky." That's all—just looking at the trees, appreciating their fundamental form, and remembering it.

But occasionally there are random entries of memories that suddenly came back to her, including one afternoon with her childhood friends, Billy and Hilda, who lived in a gypsy caravan "in a corner of a ragged field—rent free."

That day they went to a meadow along the river.

"It was a hidden away place, weedy musty, shady. But in the sunny patches were millions of yellow orange buttercups," she wrote. The children filled jars with tadpoles. When they headed home on their bikes she made the mistake of riding barefoot, which hurt her feet, slowing her down, and her friends raced ahead on the path. Soon they were out of sight and a man came out of the woods, stopping her on the pathway.

"The pedals were digging into my feet and the water was slopping out of the tadpole jar. In a flash he had me," she wrote. "I was flustered. Just a little girl, didn't know what to do. His hand flew up my clothes and he was pulling me from my bike."

Then two nurses appeared, stepping through a hidden gate in a hedge that ran along the path. The man saw them, let her go, and ran toward the river.

"The nurses were laughing and talking. They smiled at me. I dusted my feet and sandals. It was a close call... If the nurses had not been changing shift I would probably have had a different experience. I think I was eight at the time. I can still see that man who frightened me—like it was yesterday."

This was a story she never told her children. But there it was, sandwiched in between a recipe for keeping deer out of flower beds (mix eggs with water and paint the petals) and a list of favorite place names (Clutesi Road, Snowdrop Road, Marigold Road).

Among all the nature observations there was another uncharacteristic entry. Under the heading "Death," she writes of first suspecting my father was being unfaithful.

Many years after she wrote that he left her to remarry. My mother never had another romantic relationship as far as I knew. But in her field diaries there are entries that suggest otherwise. There is the man she visited by the ferry. And directly underneath a journal entry about the ditches being full of weeds, there is a photo of a man I never met or heard her speak of.

"This is Derik," her notes say. "He was a piano player. We were friends for a while. He was Welsh. And a pianist in a restaurant."

That's it. No further explanation, and now it is too late to ask.

It is hard for a son to admit that while he loved his mother, he barely knew her as anything but a mother, cast in a role so powerful there isn't space for anything else to exist. What did I really know about her? Or about my enigmatic father? Does any child really know their parents?

There are often pieces missing from even our most intimate, shared, deeply connected lives, secrets and mysteries that give us different realities. I had been such a close part of my mother's life for so long, as a child, yet as an adult found myself confused and wondering what about our relationship was real and what was dreamed. And I wondered if I was as much a cipher to my own children. I hoped not. I hoped that through the shared experience of fly fishing, through our immersion in nature, we had forged a deeper relationship, a balance, as the tide knows the sea.

———

MY MOTHER LIVED ON SALT SPRING ISLAND for many years before retiring and moving to a small apartment just outside Victoria, close to woodlands and farm fields. She went bike riding daily and once brought me a tiny, perfect hummingbird nest she had found and placed in a glass jar as a present. It looked fragile, but like her it was woven in a way that gave it a hidden strength.

She never revealed her inner world to me, never talked about herself until the very end. One day at work my phone rang in the Vancouver news bureau where I worked and my brother Andy spoke calmly, but with urgency. "Mom collapsed. You'd better come now if you can."

At Victoria General Hospital the doctor said he could find nothing wrong with her, although she had crumpled to the floor unconscious, leaving a dent in the drywall where her head struck, waking later to call Andy for help. The morning she collapsed she had just come back from a nine-mile bike ride through the countryside.

"I don't know how long she lay unconscious," Andy said. "It could have been minutes. It could have been hours."

That night my brothers Andy and Jon and I sat with her in the hospital and stories poured out of her. She talked about her childhood and ours. She told my brothers the story she'd told me years earlier of walking home from Fulford Harbour and sleeping alone in the forest. She told us she'd bought a cemetery plot and knew it was the right place because when she went to look at it, a deer was browsing on the grass among the gravestones where one day she would lie. She told stories I'd never heard before about her childhood and serving in the Land Army, once driving her bike into a ditch to avoid a German plane machine-gunning the road. The words came tumbling forth in a torrent. A rainstorm passed over the mountain and the streams flooded to life.

Lying in the hospital bed she was bright, energetic, and effervescent. The doctor wanted to keep her overnight for observation, just as a precaution, he said, and so my brothers and I went home to sleep. I told my worried daughters their gran had been hospitalized, but was okay. She had been close to them when they were small, but as they grew into young adults she drifted away. She remembered every Christmas, every Valentine's Day, every birthday they had, sending cards and presents. But her visits to them dropped off. It seemed hard for her to relate to anyone who wasn't a child. I knew she was never as happy as when she was a young mother, with her kids running wild and coming home with bird eggs, bunches of asparagus, or freshly caught trout.

She died alone in the hospital, on the night of May 24, 2008.

She had disconnected all the electronic monitors attached to her and there was no alarm when her heart stopped. The nurse found her with her hands folded on her chest, her face serene, as if she were lying in a forest glen.

I think the last thing she heard was the dawn chorus. And when the deer walked away into the woods, she followed, the ferns barely moving as she passed among them.

When we cleaned up her small apartment, emptying it for the last time, I found an old tin box for chocolates. On the lid was a painting of a speckled trout and inside were some wild bird feathers: an owl, a flicker, a hummingbird. A note said: "Mark's box—1956." That was the year I began school and went fishing for the first time. Next to the box were copies of two of my books, *Run of the River* and *River of the Angry Moon*, their covers creased from use. She had never mentioned reading them.

That night I sat with my daughters and we went through photo albums, looking at pictures of them as children with their granny. She was there with them through their preschool and kindergarten years, but her presence in the photo album faded away as they grew up, became teenagers, and went to high school.

"That seems so long ago," said Emma, looking at a picture of her and her sister as little girls, sitting with their gran in the garden, tiny cups the size of blooming flowers beside them. They were waiting to serve the faeries tea.

At my mother's funeral my brother Tim arrived with a crate, which he carried carefully. When he opened it a flock of white doves flew out. They circled high above the clearing, orienting themselves, and then they turned toward their dovecote, on Salt Spring Island.

I stood with my daughters at the graveside, thinking about the ways in which parents fail to connect with their children, about how fast the river flows, and how easily life is silenced. I had largely lost my fear of dying, of abandoning my daughters, thanks to the wisdom of a fly fishing hermit priest. Even there in the graveyard it didn't come back to haunt me. But I didn't know then about the cancer.

SWIMMING
UP

LYING ON THE GURNEY I heard a misaligned wheel clacking as we went down the hallway. Why didn't somebody fix it? The lights passed over me, hypnotic glow, white ceiling, *clack, clack,* ceiling, hypnotic glow.

We turned into a bright room and they lifted my naked body and laid me on the operating table. The surface was slightly soft and sticky so that I wouldn't slide away like a fish being gutted.

The last of my resistance, the nerve of fear, had dissolved that morning when I'd walked into the hospital knowing this would be the day. It was up to others now, and so I lay still on the operating table where a surgeon would remove my prostate, and hopefully all the cancer cells growing within it.

I went into the hospital fully formed but knew I would emerge bereft of something, cut away from myself. Still, I would be alive. I thought of it as plucking out one eye to fend off blindness in both. The surgeon sat nearby facing a screen, moving controls that silently unfolded a robotic arm that would penetrate me. A face leaned in.

"I'm the anesthesiologist," he said. "Count backwards from twenty."

I hesitated. "Twenty, nineteen, eighteen." I stopped. I couldn't recall what came next. In the darkness I could hear nurses moving. Someone was swabbing my stomach. The operating table was so adhesive I couldn't lift my arms. I felt congealed. My throat was so dry it constricted. My tongue stuck to the roof of my mouth. I desperately needed water. I forced up first one arm, pulling it free from the sticky table, then the other. I was reaching out, searching for a hand to hold so I could pull someone close and ask for help.

"Doing your swimming exercises?" A woman's voice asked close by my side. After a moment she understood, took my hand, leaned in.

"Water," I asked.

The nurse put a small, damp sponge on a stick between my lips and when I closed my mouth the water spread like illumination.

"Good?" she asked.

"Hold my hand," I asked, and she did, so I didn't drift back into darkness.

I had been there before, at that point where you feel like you are teetering on the edge of nothingness.

About twenty-five years earlier I sat in a hospital room alone after surviving a crash that ripped apart the car I was a passenger in. A friend and I were coming back from camping at Long Beach. We had been there when the humming-birds returned in the spring and we watched flocks of them zinging along a bluff to scatter in the forest around us.

On the drive home John pulled out to pass a slow car. He put his foot down, accelerating, just as a dump truck veered across the lane in front of us.

I saw the side of the truck looming like a wall, like a dam blocking a stream.

We struck the side of the truck, caromed off it, went airborne for a moment, broke an axle landing in the ditch, and tore toward the forest. I didn't hear a thing as the passenger side of the vehicle was nearly torn off. Glass sprayed across me like mist. I saw a telephone pole ahead, moving closer frame by frame, like film being jerked across a viewfinder, and I knew that if we hit it, we would stop. And we would be dead.

But the car slewed to one side, drunkenly, and the telephone pole went past us fast. The car came to a shuddering halt at the edge of the forest, a cloud of dust rising above us.

John was unhurt, except for blood pouring from his nose where a piece of whirling glass had lodged.

"Are you okay?" he asked.

"No. My side is bashed in," I said.

"Don't move. I'll get help."

"Get me out first. Get me out."

I was fighting panic. In the silence I thought I heard flames.

The right side of the car was so twisted my door wouldn't open, so John pulled me across the seat and dragged me out the driver's side.

I wasn't bleeding but soon my right hip, my stomach, rib cage, and shoulder would turn black from bruising, and I would piss blood for months.

But I was alive.

I lay by the side of the road until an ambulance arrived. I remember hearing the siren wailing far, far away. It sounded like the curfew sounding out over the dark prairie landscape, stirring the coyotes to howl.

I awoke in a hospital room before dawn. Climbed out of bed, feeling the slow ache of pain, and went to sit by the window to wait for the dawn chorus. That's when the nurse found me on her rounds. I was looking into darkness, watching the tree branches move against the streetlights, appreciating the stark beauty.

"You shouldn't be up," she said.

"I can't sleep."

"Are you in pain?"

"No, not much," I said. "Just amazed. To be alive."

She stood beside me and without saying anything, put her arm around my shoulder. I don't know if they teach nurses to do that, but of all the things they do, the affirmation of caring is among the most important.

———

THE NURSE WHO TOOK MY HAND after surgery seemed to be pulling me back into life; giving hope.

"You are going to be okay," she said as the operating technicians cleaned up around us. "It's over. The surgery went well. We are going to move you now."

Somehow it *was* over, and I hadn't even counted back to seventeen yet.

They lifted me onto the gurney. The young surgeon stood over me.

"It took longer than we anticipated," he said. "Five-and-a-half hours, not three. A bit of a marathon. You had some complications."

The prostate had an abnormal shape, he said, and so they had moved more slowly, unraveling the nerves before they

cut, hoping to maintain at least a vestigial link to my sexual-
ity, which exists not in large muscle tissue but in a sensitive
filament that reaches the brain through the central nervous
system. Break the link completely and there is no pathway
for the messages on either end to connect.

The anesthetic had worn off just moments after they
finished operating, he said, and I swam back to murky
consciousness. A nurse wheeled me away. Back down the
corridor with the same clacking wheel, the same hypnotic
lights overhead. I fell into a deep sleep. I was exhausted from
being unconscious, and I suppose because of the stress my
brain felt knowing my body was being penetrated. When I
awoke hours later, my eyes flickering open, I saw Maggie sitting next to my bed and behind her, Emma and Claire. They
were reading and had been there for hours, waiting for me
to come back to them. Claire saw my eyes.

"Mom."

In that one word I heard so much worry and fear and love
that I had to take a deep breath. Sometimes it is easier to be
the victim than the bystander. When I fought cancer, felt the
weakness and threat it spread through my body, it was my
doubt, my struggle with my disease. I could fight, but no one
else could take the burden; no one else could do anything.
All the people who loved me were helpless in the face of that
and it was painful to see how badly it wounded them.

I went home with a catheter in my urethra and a urine
bag strapped to my leg. When I peed it hurt and I felt the
urine pooling in the bag, warm against my body. There was
no dignity in that.

I lay in the bed I had shared with Maggie for so many
years and felt adrift. She lay beside me, afraid to touch my

fragile body. Drugs eased the torment, but when I closed my eyes there would be a ragged wheel of color spinning and I would jerk awake feeling nausea. I stopped taking the pills, preferring the pain, which was like gravity, holding me to the earth, to my life.

Emma and Claire came to sit with me. They brought me fly fishing magazines and said I would be ready to go out with them in the spring. But I could see fear in their eyes. Nobody knows where cancer is going to go, and they thought maybe we might never fish together again.

One day a nurse tenderly removed the catheter and unstrapped the drainage bag, and I felt for the first time I might just recover. But the pain kept jabbing at me. Some people have told me they recovered from prostate surgery in a matter of days. One woman said her husband was triathlon training within weeks of his operation. But I was devastated by it. My body ached for a month. At night I lay in bed and tried to remember sex and couldn't. The circuit board had been smashed and burned.

"You're going to be okay," Maggie said.

"No," I said. "I'm changed. I just have to accept it."

She drew up against me.

"I don't."

Emma and Claire talked to me every day, visiting me in my bedroom, where I lay for long hours. Emma was preparing to graduate from university and Claire from high school, which left them both busy and distracted. But there was in them a quiet hope, a faith I would pull through, and I couldn't imagine letting them down.

Maggie laid her head against my shoulder at night and I felt the softness of her hair and remembered lying with her in the tent at San Josef Bay, and paddling with her on the Bowron River, with the grizzly bear towering above us.

I was too weak to go camping, or to hike through the wilderness, so I made do with short walks in the city. I started by going to the end of the block, just three houses down from where we lived. Then I made it around the block.

Soon I was following a familiar route through the neighborhood, down the ravine where an owl had once swooped at me, where a pair of coyotes had a hidden den, and across the soccer fields where I had once run so fast.

It wasn't until I walked that I really felt life coming back into my body. Strength began to return, seeping in like water, as I passed under the trees, saw the miracle of their leaves, watched birds flit, and stopped to marvel at the sound of rainwater dripping down a drain. The opening words from my mother's diary came back to me: "If I can walk I'm happy."

Father Brandt had always told me to walk slowly, to walk purposefully, to stop and look at nature. Now I had no choice as I shuffled along the street, studying the gardens of my neighbors, and seeing in them how people sought to shape nature to fit their own needs. Green grass spread everywhere, like plastic carpeting, and a fleet of commercial gardening trucks patrolled the streets, with roaring lawn mowers and leaf blowers restoring neatness and maintaining order. I yearned to be somewhere wilder, but it took time to grow stronger, for the pain to ebb. I walked daily, willing myself to add a few extra steps each time I went out. At home I sat at my fly tying vice but couldn't concentrate, couldn't remember the way to tie patterns I had mastered long ago. I tried to write, but the sentences wouldn't connect; the words that could provide linkage were simply not there and there was nothing in their place but spaces. This, I thought, was what early-onset dementia must feel like, like waking in a house you don't know and which you can't remember entering.

———

THE WEEKS DRAGGED INTO MONTHS, but slowly I started to recover. The scars healed on my skin. I began to read newspapers again, focusing on the shortest reports first. When I lost the thread of a story, I went back to the beginning and began again. As my concentration improved, I read longer pieces. Later I opened a book, *Marcovaldo, or The Seasons in the City*, by Italo Calvino. It began with a line about the wind bringing "unusual gifts" from far away, in this case the spores of mushrooms. I was entranced from then until it ended, 121 pages later, with a hare escaping a wolf by disappearing into an expanse of snow as white as blank paper. Emptiness, I realized, can be a story in itself.

At the prostate clinic for a post-operative consultation I sat with a woman who had a formal title, but who referred to herself simply as "the sex nurse." Sexual dysfunction, she said, was one of the common side effects of the surgery I'd had, which is known as a radical prostatectomy.

"The severity and duration varies in patients," she said. "And some of that may be up to you, because the most important sexual organ is the brain."

We looked passively at each other across the desk.

"Since the operation," I said, "I haven't even been able to think about sex. I just can't imagine it anymore."

"Well, you are going to have to try," she said.

One day I got up, went to my vice, and tied a small, delicate fly that imitated a freshwater shrimp. It seemed perfect and I marveled at how the coding for that pattern, which I thought I'd forgotten, had been drawn from somewhere hidden in my brain. I thought, "there is residual wiring in there, you just have to find it; you have to start using it again."

I was getting better by the week, but I knew I wasn't whole and wouldn't be for a long time. The surgery had left a gap in me both physically and psychologically. Studies have shown that depressive symptoms occur at a rate four times greater in men with prostate cancer, and I could feel the darkness rising in me, the tidal shifting of despair. My self-image had been shaken, and although my prostate had been removed, I didn't know yet if the cancer was gone. Maybe, I thought, I'll never know.

THE PATH THROUGH THE FOREST

THE DARK FOREST WAS troubling when I first dreamed it in its brooding, unpredictable, unsettling stillness. It seemed almost to be crouched. As I approached I saw there was a small gap in a wall of trees, a dark opening that led within. I crossed the meadow to stand at the entrance. But once I had done that, I felt compelled to enter, to step into the uncertainty of the penumbra. As my eyes adjusted to the light, branches took shape weaving up toward the hidden sun and knotted coils of roots came into focus, reaching down into the earth. The forest was like a web, a weaving of sinuous wood, linking the sky to the ground.

There was a faint trail, but it vanished in the thicket and seemed to go nowhere. The whole place felt foreboding at first; it was a fairy-tale forest where children would wander until found by witches or wolves. Then I heard the song of a small bird falling from the dense canopy and that was, to paraphrase Leonard Cohen, the crack that let the light in. I realized the path through the forest would take me some-where if I let it, and when I awoke I wanted to go there.

The morning after that dream I rose with a sense of pur-pose. My fight with cancer, I hoped, was over. My body was still healing, still aching at times, but I wanted to come back, to wade deep in life again, and I felt I could. But I needed to go fishing alone first, the way I used to. I knew my daughters would go with me if I asked, but since the surgery I felt myself worrying I might be too weak to wade the river with them again. So I wanted to find out.

"Are you sure?" Maggie asked when I told her I was going fishing by myself.

"I am," I said, trying not to sound worried, and I could see the relief in her face, sensing someone she once knew was returning. When I drove out of the city, my fishing bag and two-handed fly rod in the back, I knew where I would go. In the dream I remembered a forest trail I'd discovered a few years earlier. It led to a place where a river came around a big bend, and pushed salmon into the shallows along a curved gravel bar.

The first time I found that path, it was dark and cold and I peered into the woods wondering what lay ahead. I hes-itated, then went on. When you fish alone it is best not to think of bears and cougars, otherwise they seem always to be lurking in the shadows, and I forced myself not to look over my shoulder as I walked through the forest. I found the river, but the salmon weren't in that day. And then I forgot about the trail for a few years. On my return visit I decided not to think of cancer.

I followed the path down a bank where the roots of great trees were exposed, and sunlight rarely reached the ground.

Then the trail led me into a thick patch of willows, where the branches interlaced and the light was soft and green. The trail emerged on a river channel that was dry, except for a small trickle of water. Soon it would pulse with water, but it was late summer now, nearly fall, and the channel wouldn't fill until October rains came. That would bring it back to life.

The salmon waited for those fall rains to lift the water level and open pathways for them into the forest. Salmon runs come in from the ocean in the fall, mostly coincident with the rains, but some arrive in the summer when water levels are low. Those fish arrive early because they are impatient, or because they know something the others don't. They hold in the main river until the downpours begin and all the small rivulets start to flow. Then they run up the tributaries to spawn.

Those waiting salmon were what I wanted to find. I knew striking just one would pull me back into life, would jolt me out of my post-hospital stupor and remind me of the joy I had once known.

Leaving the trail I followed the dry channel to where it joined the Squamish River. I felt the salmon should be close, but nature has its own schedule and one never knows for sure when the runs will arrive. When they do come in they announce themselves with splashy jumps and by tilting their heads and backs out of the water, as if looking for landmarks.

I stood on the riverbank watching for salmon, my eyes scanning the surface, but the river swept past without any sign, inscrutable. Was I too early? Or had I forgotten how to read the water?

I was separated from the main river by a side channel that was shallow and flowing quickly. It had been easy for me to wade across the last time I visited. But today I was less sure of myself; less certain of my footing. I didn't want to think as a cancer survivor, that I was too weak to wade where I once went so easily. But I was afraid of stumbling, of being beaten down by a river that should lift me, and once that thought got into my head it was hard to get it out.

Across the side channel was the wide gravel bar I wanted to reach, and beyond that, on the main river, I saw four fishermen well spaced apart, casting their flies. So the salmon must be there. I nudged into the current knee-deep, but the river seemed stronger than before, the rocks under my feet less steady, and I retreated.

None of the distant fishers were catching anything, but they were focused on a stretch of water, casting repeatedly to the same area, and their intensity told me they must see something moving, probably dark dorsal fins, or the tips of tails. That is where the salmon are schooled, I thought, a fibrillation, a living mass quivering within the steady pulse of the cold gray river. I had to go there.

I started to wade the channel again, but by the time I got waist-deep I knew the current was too strong for me. It was unrelenting. It wanted to push me to the sea. Shaken, I waded back to where I started, and sat on the riverbank waiting for something. I was not sure what. To grow stronger?

I pulled a sandwich out of my pocket and started to eat lunch, watching the river, the movement of the water, and the light. This is enough, I thought, just to be beside the river and out of my sickbed. Then a salmon rolled in the streaming, ashen water just a few yards from me, so close I could have reached out with my rod tip and touched the surface where it vanished. I watched, not sure I saw what I saw: a gray, silty back, in gray, silty water. It would be so easy to imagine that a wave was a salmon's back. Then two more salmon rolled, looping out of the water together, showing their silver sides, a glint of golden eye visible for a flash, before they sank from sight. A school of fish was moving upstream, tight to the shoreline, hidden by glacial silt. The river had brought the fish to me, delivered them to my feet.

I stood slowly, chewing the last bit of bread, and watched the water, shaking the fly line loose from my rod. The line twitched like a cat's tail. With a simple flip of the rod I lifted the fly and threw it onto the water. It sank, drifted a moment, and then the line went tight. The dream and the path through the forest had brought me to this: a salmon, fresh from the sea. I could feel the fish tugging urgently, the rod tip jumping like a needle for a cardiograph.

I stumbled after the running salmon, regaining line, then losing it again when the fish surged away, racing farther downstream. It had been over a year since I last hooked a fish and I was surprised by how strong it felt; uncontrollable. But slowly the energy began to play out as I gave and took line, with the rod absorbing the shock, until finally I brought the salmon to shore near the tail of the pool, fifty yards from where the fight started. Somehow I had run along the shore, stepping rock to rock, without falling. I held the fish for a moment. It was cold, hard, and silver and had sea lice near its tail. The parasites die in fresh water, so the salmon probably came into the river that night, while I lay in the city, dreaming.

The salmon seemed a miracle to me, and I wondered if through my hands it could feel the pulse of my heart, if it could comprehend the moment in any intelligent way.

Its gills opened and closed, showing flashes of red, and I thought of its great journey across the eternal green ocean and up the timeless gray river, its transect marked now by our encounter. It made no effort to escape until I opened my hands. Then it shot ahead and vanished. Silt into silt.

I walked slowly back upstream, cast again, and before the line had a chance to swing around another fish took, bolting forward to grab the fly. It ran upstream into fast water, then turned down, jumping as it went, flailing the surface, throwing up spray that shone in the sunlight. After a struggle I landed the salmon in quiet water. The fish and I were both tired, but it soon revived and swam away. I rested for a moment, sitting in the water in my waders, then slowly walked back upstream. I cast again. And another salmon grabbed my fly. That morning in seven casts I took five salmon. I killed the fifth, then stopped fishing.

From a dream I had awoken to a surfeit of fish. I was overwhelmed by my fortune, by the feeling of being back on the water again; by the taste of sharp, clean air and the sound of the river. I sat on the bank, a big silver fish laid out on the rocks beside me. After resting I went back into the woods thinking to head home early. But then I heard a warbler; the same bird as in my dream. Instead of turning back to the truck, I went in the other direction, deeper into the forest, pushing through a thicket of willows. I got lost momentarily, then found another trail, one I hadn't encountered before. It led to a small stream and I crossed to where boots had cut steps into a muddy bank. I climbed up and went through the trees toward the sound of the river, far away. The new path took me through groves of stately maples and rustling black cottonwoods, where sunlight spilled off high branches and fell on the alder berry bushes on the forest floor. Ahead I saw the light of the river through the trees.

I sat in deep grass on the bank to finish my lunch, wondering if there could be mountain lions in the forest, then I lay back to sleep in the sunlight that filtered through the canopy and dappled my face. The blood in my eyelids pulsed, glowed red, then faded to black. When I awoke I saw the cottonwoods leaning over me, branches spread like arms, close and protective. I followed the trail to the river and a beautiful run of water stretching a city block along a wide gravel bar. The river was as smooth as pavement, as wide as a highway, and there were several fly fishers spaced like hitchhikers along the road, casting flies to a vast school of salmon, which splashed and cleaved the water. There was a traffic jam of silver salmon off the bar, nudging bumper to bumper. Now and then an angler hooked up and a big fish peeled off line before jumping far out across the river. I waded in until the water was up to my waist, feeling the bottom cautiously with my feet, but I couldn't bring myself to go as deep as the other fly fishers, who were in up to their chests and thirty feet closer to the salmon. I cast as long a line as I could, but my fly fell short of the school of salmon, and for two hours it came back untouched. I kept hoping a fish would stray within my casting range. But when you fish there is a moment when you know it is time to stop. It just is. The last grain of sand drops and it is time to go. I sensed the end, waded back to shore, and followed the path through the forest. When I looked back I could still see the line of fly casters, throwing their lines out toward the finning salmon.

I was tempted to turn aside to fish again in the shallow side channel where I had been so lucky earlier, but I had had a perfect morning there and wanted to leave it at that. So I went on to the truck, carrying the salmon I had killed. It bumped gently against the side of my waders as I climbed the hill, passing the tendril, searching roots of a five-hundred-year-old tree.

I felt tired, but stronger somehow, uplifted. I was reconsidering life, thinking about what it means to get a second chance, about what I might change. I was pleased with the day and with knowing I could bring Emma and Claire to the side channel where I'd caught the fish, point to the bucket of water behind the rock, and hopefully guide them right to a waiting salmon. And even if the fish had moved on by then, I knew they would enjoy walking through the shadowy forest. They would cherish going from the cool darkness into the light by the river with me.

———

A FEW WEEKS LATER, on a bright fall day Claire and Emma and I drove the Sea-to-Sky Highway out of Vancouver, the remarkable, rippling beauty of Howe Sound unfolding as we headed toward the Squamish River, opaque with glacial silt, from mountains ground to flour by moving water.

Both my daughters were busy with university and building their own independent lives, and I wanted to be with them while I still could. This was our first fly fishing trip together since my operation. So it was a special day, and as we headed to the river the sun came out on the blue sea below the highway and the layered green mountains beyond.

I told them the cancer was gone, I thought, but I would be checked routinely for possible recurrence. I said in five years we will know for sure, although I knew I would never know for sure.

"I'm healing. I feel it," I said. They were silent, looking out the window at the landscape. I was happy to be with them again, heading out toward a salmon river. As we drove I talked with them for the first time about my anxieties, not just about cancer, but about my earlier fear of death and another darkness that had haunted me at times throughout my life.

"Depression is hard to understand," I said. "I have a wonderful life but this shadow intrudes sometimes. It just comes. And sometimes I feel a sense of panic, a desire to flee. I don't know from what, or what causes it. It is not rational and it makes my relationship with your mom difficult. For her it is upsetting. And it is something I am struggling to understand about myself and we have been going to a therapist for help."

It was a lot to say and I had waited too long to say it.

"I keep trying to understand it. And I think I am. If I can fight cancer I can fight this too."

That black feeling had been there off and on for a long time, I said, but I had held it in. Then cancer shook things loose in me.

"But unlike cancer, anxiety can't be cut out like unwanted tissue," I said. "So in some ways it is harder to deal with."

It was clinging to me; a feeling of failure, of ineffable sadness, a sense that everything was lost. The wave would hit the shore and subside. But I always wondered if one day it would drag me out to sea.

For a long time the therapist Maggie and I saw had wanted to put me on my own path, to find my way through the forest by talking openly about my feelings. That day as we drove to the river I was finally doing that, saying the words to two of the most important people in my life. And it felt good. It felt like I was surfacing after swimming deep under water. I didn't keep a diary the way my mother did. But had I, this would have been the moment when I handed it to my daughters and said, *here, read this.*

If my admission of struggling with depression, on top of cancer, was a shock to my daughters, it didn't show. There wasn't any awkward silence, no dismay about a strong father revealing weaknesses. No fear that their father wasn't the man they thought he was or that the relationship between their parents had weaknesses. The girls instead began talking about their own feelings, about their own self-doubts, as a way of saying: *we understand.* And in that moment I felt the unquestioning love they had for me. They were saying it was okay to be who I was, a little broken, and trying to find my way.

MY DAUGHTERS TALKED ABOUT HOW they dealt with their own stresses, about their own feelings of inadequacy, and about their deep fears for the future because of the climate crisis my generation was forcing on them. They knew the value of nature and they were struggling, they said, to understand how humanity could blindly cause so much damage. They wondered if they should have children in such a troubled, uncertain world, and that made my heart ache.

"But every generation faces an existential threat," I said. "For me it was the fear of nuclear Armageddon. At school they taught us how to hide under our desks, and I saved newspapers at home so I could cover the windows because I believed paper could stop radiation from coming through glass.

"In the past people have feared catastrophic plagues, or starvation, and at one time they thought dragons might come down from the mountains to burn their villages. It's as if people have to have something immense to fear. Maybe that shared fear holds the tribe together."

The girls listened quietly.

"But our dragons are real, not abstract, not symbolic," said Emma.

"Maybe it is human nature that we have to have something to be afraid of," said Claire. "But societal fears usually prompt meaningful action. And yet with global warming, I just don't see any action commensurate with the danger. Pipelines are still being built, oil sands are still being mined, and the planet is getting hotter and hotter."

"Yeah," I said, "but your generation is not just hoping for a better world, you are demanding it. So I hope you have kids, because your children can inherit a planet you have helped to improve."

It wasn't a very convincing argument. I knew I didn't have to fear the climate dragon because I wouldn't be around long enough to see the full damage. And the pandemic that would shake the world was still ahead of us then. On that sunny day we had no inkling of that horror.

As we talked we drove to the river and walked through the forest, on the path I'd dreamed about. I hoped the salmon would still be there and that I would be strong enough to feel comfortable wading deep in the big river.

We went through a grove of old-growth cedars and just before reaching the river we hit thickets of alder. One of the skills you have to learn as a fly fisher is how to walk through tangled brush while carrying a nine-foot rod. I threaded my way through the branches and my daughters followed without pausing, without getting their rods or lines caught in branches. It reminded me of being a boy, crawling through the bush along Penticton Creek.

We emerged on the river right where the current had earlier swung my fly into the path of migrating salmon.

"I wonder if the fish are still here," I said.

Rivers are always changing; salmon shift on a whim, water levels rise or fall, and places that should hold fish suddenly become empty. So every time you come to the river the search begins again.

"Cast into that little bucket of water behind that rock," I said.

Emma made a quick cast, and a moment after her fly landed, she hooked a bright, silver salmon. It led her down the pool, fighting all the way until she landed it. Then Claire stepped into the river, unfurled her line, and did the same thing. The salmon jumped and ran and she ran after it until it tired and came to hand.

That day the river opened itself to them. They weren't standing outside nature; they were part of it, waist-deep in it, with glacial gray water streaming around them, the sky bowing above and salmon charging to take their flies. But after they had taken several salmon their flies began to swing through the pool untouched.

"There are still fish in there," I said. "But they have been put down by all the commotion. We need to leave them now. Upstream there is a long run where I saw a big school. The fish were jammed together, but I couldn't wade deep enough to reach them. Let's give it a try."

We followed the path, and when we came out of the woods Emma and Claire stood on the gravel bar, looking at the river, seeing how it was folded into seams and how the salmon were lying far out against the main current. They read the water, then waded in as deep as they could, going deeper than I had gone last time. I stood back and watched. Their first few casts fell short. But they stretched out their lines and soon both were into fish. Both salmon jumped free, going high in the air and spinning away. A few casts later both were hooked up again; salmon were crashing after their flies, taking hard and running with the strong current.

My daughters teased one another when they were playing fish. It added to the challenge.

"Just land it already," Emma said as Claire struggled with one salmon. She had fought it to the shore, only to have it turn at the last moment and run far out into the river again. It found heavy water in the main current, and peeled off line.

"I can't get the line in. I only lift five-pound weights in my workouts," Claire said, her rod bending against the salmon, which was still surging away from her.

For a long time the fish was winning; it was too strong for Claire to stop. But she persisted, and the drag slowly wore the salmon down. Then the fish hesitated, throbbing in the current, and Claire applied pressure, wading backward toward shore, pulling the salmon with her, turning it out of the main river. A few minutes later the salmon wallowed in the shallows near her feet—but just as I got up to help land it, the hook pulled free. The salmon splashed as it escaped back to the finning school. Claire sat down in the water, her arms held up in disbelief. Such a long fight and no fish to show for it. Emma groaned.

"Played it too long," Claire said and they both laughed.

I stood on the gravel bar, watching them cast over the roiling water where salmon backs broke the surface steadily. The two young women cast smoothly, mended their lines, and got lost in the rhythm, until a salmon grabbed their fly. The fish were big and strong and fresh from the sea and through good fortune, and knowledge born from years on the water, we had come to the river as the run passed. We had stepped perfectly into nature's movement.

After a few hours the salmon stopped hitting. Then just as we were about to quit Emma hooked one last fish and played it expertly. Claire helped her land it, grasping it just above the tail and pulling it to shore.

"I want to keep this one for dinner with friends tonight," said Emma.

We carried the silver and gray salmon up onto the bank. It was the color of glacial ice. I struck it once with a piece of driftwood and the fish lay still. Emma gutted it beside the river, splashing water up on the shore to wash the stones stained with blood. Where the salmon ended its life the wet stones shone with fish scales that sparkled like flecks of minerals, like stars.

Emma washed her hands in the river before we left, the last blood drifting away in the current: this was ablution.

We sat for a moment, just listening to the river rustling past. It sounded like Claire's ballerina dress when she danced pirouettes as a girl, spinning and spinning without getting dizzy. I had been thinking of death while I walked the trail that day, not in a fearful or melancholic way, just considering its reality, turning it over in my mind. Accepting it. It had come close with cancer; it had reached out and brushed my face, then passed by, leaving me alive, if diminished. Maybe it would come again, but I felt fortunate to be out on the water and to be as close to my daughters as I had ever been. Perhaps closer, now that they were grown, and my equals in every way. Heading back up the trail, Emma carried her salmon, and I felt we had accomplished a lot more than just a good catch that day. We had gone looking for fish and had found something else, a reaffirmation of a connected life. And joy, of course.

———

A FEW WEEKS LATER, feeling optimistic about my health, sleeping better, and waking without pain, I started to think about going fishing again with Emma and Claire. I sent them a note, wondering if they could fit another trip in to their busy lives. I knew that with university graduation and jobs coming in the years ahead, they would have less time to be with me, and I wasn't sure how permanent that disconnection from me and from fly fishing might be once it happened. They binged back a response moments later. "Can't wait," wrote Emma. "I will be there," wrote Claire.

And so we went to a gentle river we had fished together when they were children. The water was clear and low in the fall, and wading was easy. But I went slowly, watching the water. When I saw a trout rise, a silver ring drifting away with the current, I told Emma, "There's one. Cast up alongside that log." I pointed with my rod tip.

"No, this one is yours," she said. "I just want to watch."

I made a cast and the fish took on the first drift. Emma splashed over in her waders and netted a bright rainbow trout for me. We admired its perfect form before tipping it out of the net. Free again.

"It feels good to be back on this little river," I said. "I have never fished up above here before. Let's go exploring."

The banks were steep and there was no trail upstream, so we waded up the middle of the river, the girls offering me an arm for support at times. In the past they had leaned on me, but they were bigger and stronger now, and I was not. The water was cold and clear and we waded waist-deep. Our dog, Sami, swam behind us, trusting we knew where we were going and glad to be out with his pack again. We went slowly, just seeing new places, and deep in the valley found a long pool so far from the road it likely hadn't been fished much.

"This is what we have been searching for," I said.

"Nice run," said Emma. "And there are fish rising along the far bank." She pointed with her rod to where trout were dimpling the surface.

I sat on a rock and watched Emma and Claire get into position and start casting to the rising trout. I had watched them as little girls struggling to use rods far too big for them, but now they were young women, graceful and able to wade where they wanted to in a wild river. Their casts were skillful and unhurried. Every now and then a small, perfect rainbow trout rose to take down one of their flies, and a commotion followed, with shouts of advice, dog barks, and laughter.

After a while the fish stopped taking the cast flies, but we could see they were still coming up for real mayflies. It was hot, a rare summerlike day in October, so we sat in our waders with our legs in the cold water while we ate lunch, watching tiny, dark mayflies dancing in the air above us. Emma searched through her fly box until she found a fly the exact color and size of the mayflies. She held it up and Claire nodded approval. Matching the hatch, they both tied on the new pattern. They soon caught a trout each and then the hatch subsided, the mayflies danced away from the water, and the fish stopped rising. The sun moved across the valley and the shadow of the mountain leaned over the forest and the river. It was all synchronous.

"Time to head back," I said, but the girls already knew and had started to wind in their lines. We waded downstream and walked through the woods, the river fading away below us.

It was a long drive home after a tiring day for me, but I knew it was important. Reconnecting on the river again was a way of affirming life, of saying, well, death was close, is always close, but we had this day. Claire sat in the back seat, the dog's head resting on her lap. Emma rode up front with me, choosing music. We liked going fishing together—but I knew on that drive home that there would be fewer days like this ahead.

BOUND
BY WATER

ONE WINTER A FEW YEARS after my operation, Claire came home from England, where she was getting her master's at the University of Cambridge. In England there was fishing available for trout at a nearby reservoir, but she hadn't met any classmates who shared her interest in fly fishing and she didn't want to go alone.

"They do fish here," she said on the phone. "But it's different. They sit in chairs on the shore along a river that is more like a canal. And I haven't seen anyone fly casting yet."

When we visited her she took us for bike rides along the River Cam, where people punted romantically in prams, toured in live-aboard barges, and raced past in sleek rowing sculls. On the path she chatted with men in folding chairs, who sat huddled, watching their baited lines dangling in dull, quiet waters.

"Any luck?" she'd ask, and they would happily recount their catch numbers, or give explanations as to why they weren't catching anything. The weather was a frequent excuse: too cold, too warm, too windy, too calm.

"Sometimes little perch. Sometimes a pike. But I never saw anyone with a trout, or a salmon," said Claire as we rode along the river.

She didn't fish at all, instead pouring herself into her studies, and I wondered if she was leaving it behind, if maybe this was a break that would last and fly fishing would become something she used to do in childhood, with her dad.

When she came home for Christmas it was very late in the season to find fish, but my nephew Judah, who had been working as a guide that year, said he knew where a late run of coho might be found.

Claire was keen to go, even though I said our chances of a fish were poor, so we set out one cold, wet morning, driving out of Vancouver to the Harrison River. We were the only truck at the pullout, and as the rain started to lash down we found Claire had forgotten her raincoat. She tore a hole in a plastic garbage bag and pulled it over her head, wearing it like a poncho. We set off, with curtains of mist catching in the forlorn branches of the gigantic black cottonwoods along the river.

We waded down a channel toward the main stem of the river, with coho sometimes scattering before us in the shallows. Claire fished a purple and blue fly we had tied the night before as we sat together and talked about the pressures of attending university and the stress of dealing with a fellow student, from Russia, who was harassing her. He sometimes blocked the door when she entered class and pointedly sat beside her, silent and staring. It got so bad she was avoiding common spaces where she thought she might encounter him. I asked her if I should complain to the dean.

"No," she said. "I will do that." But I could tell she didn't want to, and I worried. The course load was heavy too. Demanding. Unrelenting.

"Sometimes I feel overwhelmed," she said and I braced myself for an announcement.

"You know," I said after a long silence. "You can always quit if it becomes too much."

She looked up from the vice.

"No. I can't do that," she said. "No quitting."

She finished off her salmon fly and when I woke her the next morning, she was ready to go fishing.

Rain pounded down, relentless, unflagging, cold and saturating.

"A river, flowing from the sky to the ground," I said, looking up into the falling rain. As we walked to the Harrison it felt like the whole world was made of moving water, and we were adrift within it. We followed a narrow channel toward the main river and when it deepened we started to swing our flies ahead of us in the current, casting to the far bank and letting the force of the flow sweep them back across the stream to us. Claire was casting and wading down, and I watched to see if she needed any reminders on how to throw a line. But she picked it up smoothly again after her long break. She remembered it all.

Claire fell into an easy rhythm, swinging her fly and stepping down to cast again. I knew she was expecting nothing really and had entered what psychologists call the flow state, where an experience becomes so immersive that it is the only thing that exists. Just casting and breathing and listening to the rain spatter on the trees as the downpour slowed.

In one pool we saw the backs of several coho breaking the surface repeatedly in dark water beside a tangled root wad. There were two or three fish there, but the water was complicated. Claire would have to drop her fly near the roots, then quickly throw a loop of line upstream, mending so the fly would have time to sink before the current pulled it away from where the salmon lay.

It was going to be a tricky cast. Willows leaned over the stream, leaving only a narrow gap for a back cast. I told her to turn her head to watch the line as it went behind her, the way she had when she was first learning to cast, so that she could track the line and keep it in the corridor between the bushes.

"Think of it as casting in a church," I said. "And you want to keep the line between the pews."

She lifted the line from the water, threw it up over her right shoulder, between the branches, and with one quick false cast, shot it forward toward the roots. The fly fell perfectly, and then with a quick upward flick of her wrist, she mended the line, sending a loop upstream. The blue-and-purple fly she'd tied the night before sank, and I could see it swimming down into the black water. When the strike came it was so violent it jerked the rod tip down hard against the surface. "Whoa," said Claire, lifting sharply to set the hook. The rod bowed as the salmon tried to pull her into the pool.

A wild coho is not an easy fish to land. The fish ripped downstream, then turned and came back up, with glints of dull silver underwater. It went bank to bank, the surge of its movement creating waves in the pool. I didn't know what advice to give. Everything was happening so fast the situation seemed hopeless, with the root wad just waiting to tangle the line, and all Claire could do was hang on and wait for the inevitable. Judah ran down to help and told her to start moving upstream, wading mid-current.

"Just back up slowly and pull the salmon with you," he said. "It will follow."

As she moved upstream, the coho came along with her, and soon it was thrashing in shallower water. Judah tailed the salmon, the way good guides do, with a quick, clean grab on the narrow part of the fish's body just above the caudal fin.

When Claire took the salmon from him she kept it in the water, with one hand gripping it just above its tail, the other cradled under its belly. She held it facing into the current, more than twelve pounds of muscled salmon, its sides brushed with red, its head and back green, its gills pulsing as it gulped in water. Its colors and hooked jaw with black gums marked it as a male coho, ready to spawn.

"It's like a Christmas decoration," said Claire.

Its huge mouth gaped and Claire pulled the fly loose, being careful to keep her fingers away from the sharp, exposed teeth. When she released her grip, the salmon darted away, its big tail beating the water, sending spray into her face.

The rain had stopped briefly but soon it began to hiss down again, and Claire was cold and wet when we got back to the truck, her hands white and numb. We peeled off the plastic bag and she emerged laughing, amazed to have caught such a great fish. One salmon, five hours of freezing, torrential rain—and pure joy. She was caught. She had become a fly fisher just as her sister had, initiated by a big fish. She was no longer a child, following a father wherever he led, but an adult, going fly fishing because on a winter's day, atmospheric rivers and big, wild salmon are worth knowing about.

We sat inside the truck, the heater going full blast, and drank coffee until we all stopped shivering and I was warm enough to drive.

CLAIRE WENT BACK TO UNIVERSITY after Christmas and was soon making plans for the career that would follow. Emma had left home to attend law school at the University of Victoria a few years earlier. But she wasn't far from Vancouver, and we could still see each other for weekend fishing trips, so the separation hadn't felt that acute.

But when I watched Claire go that winter, walking away at the airport to board a flight to England, I felt the distance that would lie between us and the emptiness of the two bedrooms that now stood vacant at home. I tried to smile, tried to wave casually, knowing after graduation she would not come home to live with us again.

I felt numb, as if something vital had been bled out of me. This was one of "the scorching ordeals" that C. Day-Lewis described in "Walking Away," a poem about how a father experiences separation as his son goes off to school.

Claire, tall and elegant, moved assuredly as she eddied through the throng at the airport, a young woman bound for her future. I watched her until she vanished through security into the international departure lounge. I was trying not to let it show, but I felt untethered and reached for Maggie to stop the drift. Emma had gone, and now this. I knew that this parting, this scorching, marked the end of something and the start of something else for me as a father. But what?

Whatever our relationship was becoming, it would never be as it was.

I remembered Emma first stepping away toward adulthood on that windswept beach at Hesquiat. The storm stirred the sea and the whale bone was lifted out of the bay. It was carried to camp and set by the fire, but the rib could never find the living whale again. As we watched Claire leave I found myself hoping that as parents we had given our daughters enough. Wisdom. Resilience. Self-confidence. That's what I hoped they had. That, and a good back cast.

Returning to university Claire wrote her thesis and filed a complaint with the dean's office that forced the man who had been harassing her to cease contact. The next time I saw Claire was at her graduation ceremony at Cambridge. She wore black robes for the ancient, dignified ritual and I thought of her draped in a plastic garbage bag, her arms up fighting a wild Pacific salmon on the Harrison River, as the sky dashed itself against the mountains. She subdued the powerful fish, then cradled it in her hands, and let it go. That in a way was a degree ceremony too, a passage in the art and craft of fly fishing.

———

FIFTY-TWO YEARS AFTER I'D SLEPT in the back of my father's Ford Falcon station wagon on my sixteenth birthday, the fly rod I'd just got for a present beside me, I returned alone to Muir Creek.

In the morning when I awoke I would celebrate my sixty-eighth birthday by fishing again the waters where I had made my first, fumbling fly casts.

I parked in a clearing next to blackberry bushes, where my father's car had been parked that night so many years earlier.

Waking in the early morning darkness I clambered stiffly out, pulled on my waders and felt-soled boots. I didn't wade in runners and jeans anymore because the cold water left my joints aching. Going into the stream just below the highway bridge, I worked my way downstream, my feet pulling out of muck where, as a boy, I had walked on clean gravel. I waded knee-deep in the stream across from the old logging pylons where I had caught my first trout on a fly. I could easily cast across the stream now, gracefully and with precision, where I had once flailed the water.

I waited for the tide to turn, but it didn't bring any sea trout with it. The water rose, the surface slick and unmarked as far as I could see. There were no trout swirling, no delicate rises.

After the tide peaked, I kept wading down toward the mouth, pushing through tangled, black branches along the shore and slipping in the mud. It was like stumbling through a graveyard, and I half expected to encounter witches.

Walking north on the beach along a kelp bed where as a boy I had seen salmon swirl, I found a freshly cut road coming down the steep hillside above. A heavy machine had bulldozed through the forest to just above the beach, where winter storms had recorded the high-water mark by piling up a gravel berm. It appeared that someone was planning to build houses on the edge of the wild beach, off which I had seen killer whales hunt. One summer a pod of orcas chased a school of coho along the shore and into the creek, a murmuration of bright silver salmon fleeing into the shallows, the black-and-white whales pushing waves ahead of them before turning back to deeper water. One salmon raced upstream and frantically beached itself on a gravel bar. I picked it up later and we had it for dinner that night.

Past where the new road came down to the beach the forest was still thick, green, and moist; clear water dripped from tendrils of roots hanging off a cliff face. Twenty-five-million-year-old clamshells were embedded in the sandstone, and looking up at the record of an ancient seabed I felt afloat in time. A belted kingfisher brought me back, alighting on a cupped tree branch nearby. It was a male bird with his blue crest on display. He rattled and then looped off along the beach.

Ebbing over the sea were cirrocumulus clouds set like ridges of sand against a sky as blue as the kingfisher's back. Every part of nature fit with precision, except for the jarring scar left by the road, the road to the cul-de-sac in the rainforest. I feared houses would follow. And people would sit inside, enjoying the view, as they did on Penticton Creek, and on the other salmon beaches and rivers I first fished as a boy. "Isn't it beautiful," they would say, not knowing what had been lost.

Once as a teenager I hitchhiked to Sooke and slept alone on this beach, under a driftwood lean-to, listening to the waves close by all night. The next morning, alone in the wild as dawn arrived, I hooked a thirty-pound Chinook on a fly. I didn't land that massive fish, but we fought for a long, long time, until my arms ached. I drew the fish to within ten feet of shore, then it turned, massive and silver in the blue water, and ran away with relentless, unstoppable power. I broke off intentionally, holding the line tight until it snapped at the hook, fearing if I didn't the fish would take not just my fly, but all the expensive fly line on my reel as well.

Sometimes fish win and that's a good thing.

But the people who build houses on that beach, cutting roads and building sites in the forest, will not know about that, will not know what's been lost. They will not see the erosion of nature which they will have helped cause.

After hiking the beach I walked back to the mouth of Muir Creek and went upstream, back toward the parking lot. The path was lined with Himalayan blackberry bushes and Scotch broom, invasive plants that spread where they wanted. I met two young mothers taking their kids for a stroll, sweet and cheerful, and an older woman going to the beach to gather seaweed for her garden. She looked at me over her glasses, a pleasant, tanned face, asked about the fishing and remarked on the beauty around us. Fifty years ago, I wanted to say, it was wild here and schools of sea-run cutthroat used to come in with the tide. But instead I just smiled, nodded, and walked on.

Sitting in the sun I answered my phone to hear my daughters and Maggie calling with birthday wishes. They were all working and jealous I was out on the water. I told them the stream I knew as a boy had changed, but I still recognized parts of it.

"No trout, though," I said.

"Keep trying, Dad," said Emma. "There might be one waiting for you."

Later I went to search above the bridge and found a bend in the stream where, five decades earlier, a steelhead had surfaced to snap at my fly with an audible click of its jaws. But the run of water that had once held a perfect silver bullet of a fish was now filled with silt, flushed down from the logged mountains. There was nowhere for a steelhead to hold.

Walking to the pool above I passed through a grove of old trees that miraculously had escaped logging all these years and still stood, stately elders, beside the stream. I rested my hand against one. When I first came to that pool as a boy I stood beside that same tree and watched a big sea-run cut-throat resting in front of a boulder. When I drifted my fly toward it, a second, smaller trout raced in and hooked itself, thrashing the water and scaring the bigger fish away. There was such bounty then, but now nothing stirred.

Standing on that empty pool which had once held steel-head, salmon, and sea trout and where in all my visits as a boy I never saw another angler, I understood how much of my world, how much of nature, had been lost in a single generation, that Haig-Brown's warnings had all been realized, but perhaps more fully and sooner than he ever imagined they would.

As I waded back downstream I was praying for change, wishing for the sea run cutthroat to come in again with the tide, for the steelhead and salmon to return to rivers and small streams all along the West Coast. But I knew that wouldn't happen unless people heard Father Brandt's message and learned to look on nature with love, to feel its sacredness.

———

SPIRITUALISM FOR SOME IS REVEALED in a bible, but for others it lies in the cast fly, or in the eye of a fish cradled in their hands. In such moments it is possible to experience a meditative state, to reenter the natural world, to understand again how the Earth dreams. And that is worth knowing, worth teaching.

When I became a father it was understood I would initiate my daughters into the realm of fly fishing. I would be their guide and offer them what Father Brandt described as "a way of knowing the Earth and its plan."

I had learned fly fishing the hard way, alone. But I gave my daughters the opportunity to follow me onto the water if they so chose. When they were small I helped dress them in bulky waders and felt-soled boots. I taught them how to cast, how to wade rivers, how to release fish unharmed and how to kill them. Yes, that too. What I couldn't teach them was to love the water and the cast fly. That was their choice alone. It would be their calling, or not.

Emma and Claire are grown into young women now. They enjoy fishing but they don't dream about it the way I do. They don't look at the mountains the way I do and wonder obsessively about the ribbons of blue water that flow between them.

Much of the value to them in fly fishing is the connection it gives them to each other, and to their father. Often when we are out they walk together, laughing and talking about whatever young women do, while I study the water.

They don't see as I do the slight ripples where the surface inflection indicates a fish is passing, just hidden from sight, but not quite.

They don't read the water as deeply or as quickly as I do—but they grasp the thread of the river's story, and they love reading it with me, figuring it out together.

Teaching them to fly fish was important to me, not so much because I wanted their company on the water, but because I knew it would shape their character and draw them closer to nature.

What I didn't anticipate was how much sharing fly fishing with them would mean to me. It became the most important bonding force in our relationship; it became the thing we did together, often for days at a time, in raw weather and in sunshine. It became the place we talked about life and death, about blood knots, fly patterns, and the teachings of a hermit priest.

It can be said that the line that connects us is cast—and in the casting is magic.

———

THE BIRTH OF MY DAUGHTERS changed me, as witnessing a miracle will change anyone, but so too did fly fishing with them, sharing the silence of nature with them, and watching them grow from girls into young women.

When you see someone's first breath, catch them after their first step, hear their first words, experience their first heartbreak, and realize you can't always protect them, every year is a wonder; beautiful, unexpected, and inexplicable.

To that I could add the joy of watching them make their first casts with a fly rod, wade their first rivers, catch their first trout—and release their first fish alive.

There was too, almost from the beginning but growing with time, a sense of impending loss, a realization that this could not last, that the forward momentum of their lives would eventually take them away, into their own separate places as adults.

I recognize that we are bound together, not only by blood, but by water too. But rivers flow on. And nothing, not rocks, not mountains, stops the movement until the ocean is reached and then the flow becomes something greater.

This separation of child from parent is one of the old stories of life, of course. But when it happens to you it is a new tragedy. One day the cradle lies empty. The child leaves home, and that goodbye, standing in an empty doorway, or surrounded by strangers at a busy airport, is over in moments and never over.

I sensed the inevitability of that and hoped, however, that fly fishing would remain a link between them and between us as father and daughters.

And I had faith that fly fishing made them stronger.

Several years after Claire left home she wrote a Father's Day note to assure me it had.

"Fishing with you has taught me how to be quiet and still and to watch the world around me," she wrote. "It has taught me how to be curious because there is always something new and interesting to see in nature. And though I'll never enjoy killing a fish or prying out a deeply set hook, it has taught me how to be brave and self-sufficient. It has also taught me how to outfish overly confident men."

Included with the card was a small blue-and-green trout fly she had tied.

Fathers and daughters don't always have easy relationships, but ours has been and I think it is because we have a shared wonder for the virtues of nature. When people say to me, "Your girls turned out so well," I acknowledge their mother deserves the praise for that, and I struggle to think of something I can take credit for in parenting. The one thing I did contribute was an introduction to fly fishing and the natural world it encompasses. Parents, friends, family, and teachers all shape character, but so too do wild rivers, remote mountain lakes, and big fish.

Sometimes now I will get a text from Emma that she has tapped out in a free minute at the busy law firm where she works, representing Indigenous communities fighting for environmental reparation.

"Let's go fishing," she will write, and we make plans to slip away to a trout stream or salmon river.

Claire works in developing environmental policy and protecting human rights for the province of BC. She lives in Victoria, the city where I first began fly fishing as a boy. She visits the sea-run cutthroat streams and salmon rivers I explored decades earlier and sometimes calls for advice on what patterns to use. Because of a decline in stocks, she doesn't go on the water now with the same great expectations of catching fish that I had then. But she enjoys knowing she is wading the waters of my childhood, connecting to my past, and always hopes to catch a trout or salmon where I did. She ties her own flies and has a rack of fly rods.

As I finished the final draft of this book, Emma and Claire announced they were both pregnant. They were due to give birth in the fall, just a few weeks apart, when the leaves turn color and the salmon return from the sea. They still had fears about climate change, about the destructive foolishness of humanity, but they had come to believe in the future of the world. Through nature they had found faith.

When I put my arms around them now I feel the strength in their shoulders and think of how I used to cradle them as babies, afraid they might fall. Now I lean on Emma and Claire for support when I feel broken, when we wade in deep rivers.

I sense in them calmness, shaped by the water, by the silence of lakes in the morning mist, and by the song of the river in the dark forest. I see not just the young women before me, but their raucous births, breathtaking in their cardinal beauty, their faltering steps as infants, the glimmering moments when their ideas formed into words and they began to question the universe, their first perfect casts and the looks of wonder on their faces as they held trout and salmon, slick and cold in their hands. I see not just fully formed women, but the continuum of their lives spilling forth, and their future as mothers, who will one day wade streams with their own children, teaching them to cast and to read the water.

It is dawn. I awake feeling I am finally walking the path to everywhere that Father Brandt told me of, and far in the distance I hear the sacred river we both know. I turn my left hand in the light, looking for the cicatrix, the small, white scar near the inside knuckle of my middle finger. It is still there, faint but barely legible, a fish skeleton, a memory.

ACKNOWLEDGMENTS

THROUGHOUT THE BOOK quotes attributed to Father Charles Brandt are used with his permission, which he gave me in 2020, a few months before his death.

The themes in the chapters "The Watershed," "Easter Blessing," and "Where the River Leads" are developed from much shorter essays which first appeared on my blog, *A River Never Sleeps*, which is no longer posted.

Stoney Creek, described in the chapter "Catch and Release," is a pseudonym for a stream I wish to protect. The names of some lakes, and the location of the camp in Hesquiat, are left obscure for the same reason.

Events related in the chapters "Saint Joseph" and "Hesquiat" are compressed from more than one trip, but happened as described.

The Fresh-water Fishes of British Columbia, Handbook No. 5, by G. Clifford Carl and W. A. Clemens, contains black-and-white illustrations by Frank L. Beebe, and presents six color paintings of game fish without any attribution. The softcover handbook was published by the BC Provincial

Museum in 1948 and the lack of artistic credit appears to be just an oversight. *The Trout and Other Game Fishes of British Columbia*, by J. R. Dymond, published by Canada's Department of Fisheries in 1932, contains the same color plates as the BC Museum handbook, and credits them to E. B. S. Logier, Royal Ontario Museum.

OTHER BOOKS BY MARK HUME

Trout School: Lessons From a Fly-Fishing Master
(with Mo Bradley)

River of the Angry Moon: Seasons on the Bella Coola
(with Harvey Thommasen)

Adam's River: The Mystery of the Adams River Sockeye

The Run of the River: Portraits of Eleven
British Columbia Rivers

AND WITH CONTRIBUTIONS TO

Birds of the Raincoast: Habits and Habitat

Northern Wild: Best Contemporary Canadian
Nature Writing

Genius of Place: Writing About British Columbia